Laptops and Tablet PCs with Microsoft® Windows® XP Step by Step: Keep in Touch and Stay Productive—At Work, At Home, and On the Go!

Andrew Fuller

Ravipal Soin

PUBLISHED BY
Microsoft Press
A Division of Microsoft Corporation
One Microsoft Way
Redmond, Washington 98052-6399

Library of Congress Control Number 204114395

Printed and bound in the United States of America.

1 2 3 4 5 6 7 8 9   QWT   9 8 7 6 5 4

Distributed in Canada by H.B. Fenn and Company Ltd.

A CIP catalogue record for this book is available from the British Library.

Microsoft Press books are available through booksellers and distributors worldwide. For further information about international editions, contact your local Microsoft Corporation office or contact Microsoft Press International directly at fax (425) 936-7329. Visit our Web site at www.microsoft.com/learning/. Send comments to *mspinput@microsoft.com*.

Microsoft, ActiveSync, ActiveX, ClearType, Hotmail, Microsoft Press, MSN, OneNote, Outlook, PowerPoint, Windows, Windows Media, and Windows Mobile are either registered trademarks or trademarks of Microsoft Corporation in the United States and/or other countries.

The example companies, organizations, products, domain names, e-mail addresses, logos, people, places, and events depicted herein are fictitious. No association with any real company, organization, product, domain name, e-mail address, logo, person, place, or event is intended or should be inferred.

Acquisitions Editor: Hilary Long
Project Editor: Sandra Haynes
Editorial and Production: Online Training Solutions, Inc.

Body Part No. X10-95232

Contents

What do you think of this book?
We want to hear from you!

Microsoft is interested in hearing your feedback about this publication so we can continually improve our books and learning resources for you. To participate in a brief online survey, please visit: *www.microsoft.com/learning/booksurvey/*

Contents

Foreword

Mobile PCs are the fastest growing computing segment today, and for good reason: we're rapidly approaching the era of the *truly personal* computer! In this exciting future, laptops become more mobile, but also more personal than today's cellular phones. They'll be useful for more hours of your work and play life. This transformation can be seen in the decreasing size and weight of mobile PCs and increasing battery life. Just as important, however, are the advances in human/computer interfaces for handwriting and voice recognition in Tablet PC products.

We're proud of the work we have done to make Microsoft Windows XP and Windows XP Tablet PC Edition great operating systems for mobile PCs. This work constitutes steps toward truly personal computing. Please join us on this journey!

–Bill Mitchell, Corporate Vice President, Mobile Platforms Division

Acknowledgments

Without the help and support of several people this book wouldn't have happened. First, we would like to thank Andrew Dixon and Darin Fish for helping kick things off. Thanks to Hilary Long and Sandra Haynes for their patience in dealing with a couple of busy Program Managers and for guiding us though the process of writing a book.

Special thanks go to Armelle O'Neal who worked with us every step of the way and who turned our turgid text into readable prose. We couldn't have done this without her.

Windows is such a fantastic product and the experience working with folks working on this product is a reward in itself — we would like to thank these people for helping to create easy to use products and making our jobs as authors easier. Numerous other people helped us so many times that we've lost track — if you remember helping us, thank you.

And thanks to you for reading this book. We hope that you learn something new about Windows and how you can get the most out of your laptop or Tablet PC.

Finally, a personal note:

A.F. — Thanks to Shelly for her love, patience, and understanding during all the late nights it took to write this book. I can say beyond doubt that without your support I would never have been able to do it.

R.S. — Thankful beyond measure to Anupreet and respected families for their patience with the stress and long hours needed to make this book a reality and for giving me invaluable ideas about what to write.

Getting Help

Every effort has been made to ensure the accuracy of this book and the contents of its CD-ROM. If you run into problems, please contact the appropriate source for help and assistance.

Getting Help with This Book and Its CD-ROM

If your question or issue concerns the content of this book or its companion CD-ROM, please first search the online Microsoft Press Knowledge Base, which provides support information for known errors in or corrections to this book, at the following Web site:

www.microsoft.com/learning/support/

If you do not find your answer in the online Knowledge Base, send your comments or questions to Microsoft Learning Technical Support at:

mspinput@microsoft.com

Getting Help with Microsoft Windows XP

If your question is about Microsoft Windows XP, and not about the content of this Microsoft Press book, first consult the Microsoft Windows XP Help and Support Center. If you do not find your answer in the Windows XP Help and Support Center, please search the Windows XP Product Support Center or the Microsoft Knowledge Base at:

support.microsoft.com

In the United States, Microsoft software product support issues not covered by the Microsoft Knowledge Base are addressed by Microsoft Product Support Services. The Microsoft software support options available from Microsoft Product Support Services are listed at:

support.microsoft.com

Outside the United States, for support information specific to your location, please refer to the Worldwide Support menu on the Microsoft Product Support Services Web site for the site specific to your country:

support.microsoft.com

Using the Book's CD-ROM

The CD-ROM inside the back cover of this book contains all the practice files you'll use as you work through the exercises in this book. By using practice files, you won't waste time creating samples files and folders—instead, you can jump right in and concentrate on learning how to get the most out of your laptop or Tablet PC with Microsoft Windows XP. This book's CD-ROM also includes valuable resources and downloads for your mobile PC, along with a selection of electronic books (eBooks) to help you get the most out of your computing experience.

The CD-ROM for this book does not contain the Windows XP operating system. You should purchase and install that operating system before using this book.

Minimum System Requirements

To use this book, your computer should meet the following requirements:

- **Computer/Processor** Computer with a Pentium 133-megahertz (MHz) or higher processor

- **Memory** 64 MB of RAM

- **Hard Disk** Hard disk space requirements will vary depending on configuration; custom installation choices might require more or less hard disk space.

  For the eBooks and downloads, we recommend 250 MB of available hard disk space with 115 MB on the hard disk where the operating system is installed.

This book includes instructions for installing Microsoft Windows XP Service Pack 2 (SP2). The SP2 installation process requires up to 1700 MB of available hard disk space.

- **Operating System** Microsoft Windows XP Home Edition, Microsoft Windows XP Professional, Microsoft Windows XP Tablet PC Edition, or Microsoft Windows XP Media Center Edition

- **Drive** CD-ROM or DVD-ROM drive

- **Display** Super VGA (800×600) or higher-resolution monitor with 256 colors

- **Optional Applications** Microsoft Office XP, Microsoft Office System 2003, or later

Installing the Practice Files

You must install the practice files on your hard disk before you can use them in the chapters' exercises. Follow these steps to prepare the CD's files for your use:

● Insert the CD-ROM into the CD-ROM drive of your computer.

An End User License Agreement appears. Follow the on-screen directions. It is necessary to accept the terms of the license agreement to use the practice files. After you accept the license agreement, a menu screen appears.

If the menu screen does not appear, start Windows Explorer. In the left pane, locate the icon for your CD-ROM drive, and click this icon. In the right pane, double-click the StartCD executable file.

1 Click **Install Practice Files**.

2 Click **Next** on the first screen, select **I accept the terms in the license agreement**, and then click **Next**.

3 Click **Next**, and then click **Install**.

4 After the practice files have been installed, click **Finish**.

Within the installation folder are subfolders for each chapter in the book, as indicated in "Using the Practice Files."

Using the Practice Files

Each exercise is preceded by a paragraph or paragraphs that list the files needed for that exercise and explain any preparation you need to take care of before you start working through the exercise, as shown here:

BE SURE TO log on to Windows and have an active Internet connection available before beginning this exercise.

USE the *Yearly Sales Presentation* file located in the *My Documents\Microsoft Press\Laptops and Tablet PCs with Windows XP SBS\AtHome\FileTransfer* folder.

The following table lists the folders that contain each chapter's practice files.

Chapter	Folder	Subfolder
Chapter 1: Running Microsoft Windows XP on a Mobile PC	No practice files	
Chapter 2: Getting to Know Your Mobile PC Hardware	Hardware	UsingTabletPC Pen
Chapter 3: Introduction to Networking	No practice files	

Chapter	Folder	Subfolder
Chapter 4: Using Your Mobile PC at Your Desk	Working	SendingFiles
Chapter 5: Using Your Mobile PC in Meetings	Presentations	UsingPresenter
	Presentations	SharingData
	Presentations	TakingNotes
	Presentations	UsingCatalogs
Chapter 6: Using Your Mobile PC at Home	AtHome	FileTransfer
Chapter 7: At Home: Playing and Sharing Digital Media	No practice files	
Chapter 8: Traveling with Your Mobile PC	No practice files	
Chapter 9: Maintaining and Protecting Your Mobile PC	No practice files	

Uninstalling the Practice Files

After you finish working through this book, you can uninstall the practice files.

If you saved any files outside the *My Documents\Microsoft Press\Laptops and Tablet PCs with Windows XP SBS* folder, they will not be deleted by the following uninstall process; you will have to manually delete them.

Follow these steps to uninstall the practice files:

1   Click **Start**, and then click **Control Panel**.

2   In Control Panel, click **Add or Remove Programs**, and then, if necessary, click **Remove a Program**.

3   In the list of installed programs, click **Laptops and Tablet PCs with Microsoft Windows XP Step by Step**, and then click the **Remove** button.

4   Click **Yes** when the confirmation dialog box appears.

5   After the files are uninstalled, close the **Add or Remove Programs** dialog box and **Control Panel**.

If you need additional help installing or uninstalling the practice files, please see "Getting Help" earlier in this book. Microsoft Product Support Services does not provide support for this book or its CD-ROM.

Conventions and Features

You can save time when you use this book by understanding how the *Step by Step* series shows special instructions, keys to press, buttons to click, and so on.

Convention	Meaning
1 **2**	Numbered steps guide you through hands-on exercises in each topic.
●	A round bullet indicates an exercise that has only one step.
(CD icon)	This icon at the beginning of a chapter reminds you to install the files used in the exercises.
Tip	These paragraphs provide a helpful hint or shortcut that makes working through a task easier.
Important	These paragraphs point out information that you need to know to complete the procedure.
Troubleshooting	These paragraphs show you how to fix a common problem that might prevent you from continuing with the exercise.
⊠ Close	When a button is referenced in a topic, a picture of the button appears in the left margin.
Alt + Tab	A plus sign (+) between two key names means that you must hold down the first key while you press the second key. For example, "Press Alt + Tab" means "hold down the Alt key while you press the Tab key."
Black bold characters	In steps, program features that you click or press are shown in black bold type.
Blue italic characters	Terms explained in the glossary are shown in blue italic type.
Blue bold characters	Text that you are supposed to type appears in blue bold type in the procedures.
Italic characters	Folder paths, URLs, and emphasized words appear in italic type.
BE SURE TO	These words are found at the beginning of paragraphs preceding or following step-by-step exercises. They point out items you should check or actions you should carry out either before beginning an exercise or after completing an exercise.

Conventions and Features

Convention	Meaning
USE OPEN	These words are found at the beginning of paragraphs preceding step-by-step exercises. They draw your attention to practice files that you'll need to use in the exercise.
CLOSE	This word is found at the beginning of paragraphs following step-by-step exercises. They give instructions for closing open files or programs before moving on to another topic.
BE SURE TO	These words are found at the beginning of paragraphs preceding or following step-by-step exercises. They point out items you should check or actions you should carry out either before beginning an exercise or after completing an exercise.
	This icon is used to identify content that applies specifically to Tablet PCs.

Quick Reference

Chapter 1   Running Microsoft Windows XP on a Mobile PC

Page 2   **To determine what version of Windows XP you are running**

1   Click **Start**, and then click **My Computer**.

2   In the My Computer window, click **Help**, and then click **About Windows**.

3   **To download and install Service Pack 2 and all high priority updates**

1   Click **Start**, point to **All Programs**, and then click **Windows Update**.

2   On the Windows Update home page, click the **Express Installation** link.

3   Review the list of high priority updates, and then click **Install**.

4   When prompted to accept the license agreement, read the agreement, and then, if you accept the agreement conditions, click **Yes**.

5   When prompted to restart your computer, click **Restart Now**.

4   **To specify when you want to install updates**

1   Click **Start**, click **Control Panel**, and then click **Security Center**.

2   In Windows Security Center, click **Automatic Updates**.

3   In the **Automatic Updates** dialog box, make sure that the **Automatic (recommended)** option is selected and specify the time and frequency for installation of the updates you want to receive.

4   To apply the changes, click **OK**.

Chapter 2   Getting to Know Your Mobile PC Hardware

Page 12   **To view your ClearType settings and turn on ClearType**

1   Click **Start**, click **Control Panel**, and then click **Appearance and Themes**.

2   In the **Appearance and Themes** window, click **Display**.

3   In the **Display Properties** dialog box, click the **Appearance** tab, and then click the **Effects** button.

4   In the **Effects** dialog box, select the **Use the following method to smooth edges of screen fonts** check box, click **ClearType** in the drop-down list, and then click **OK**.

5   In the **Display Properties** dialog box, click **OK**.

23 **To display the current date in a ToolTip**

- Using the Tablet pen, hover the pointer over the time in the notification area.

23 **To display the Date and Time Properties dialog box**

- In the notification area, double-tap the time.

23 **To display the Display Properties dialog box**

- While hovering over the desktop, press and hold the button located on the side of your Tablet pen, and then tap **Properties**.

25 **To adjust the screen orientation to its default sequence, or to test the screen orientation sequence**

- In the notification area, tap the **Change tablet and pen settings** icon, and then tap **Change screen orientation**.

25 **To configure the screen orientation sequence**

1 In the notification area, tap the **Change tablet and pen settings** icon, and then tap **Properties**.

2 In the **Tablet and Pen Settings** dialog box, tap the **Display** tab.

3 In the **Screen Orientation** area, tap the **Change** button.

4 In the **Orientation Sequence Settings** dialog box, tap the **2** arrow, and then tap **Secondary Landscape**.

5 Tap the **3** arrow, and then tap **Primary Portrait**.

6 To close the open dialog boxes and apply the new settings, double-tap **OK**.

27 **To enable your computer to hibernate**

1 Click **Start**, click **Control Panel**, and then click **Performance and Maintenance**.

2 In the Performance and Maintenance window, click **Power Options**.

3 In the **Power Options** dialog box, click the **Hibernate** tab.

4 Select the **Enable Hibernate** check box and then click **OK**.

3 In the **Screen resolution** area, drag the slider to the right to change the screen resolution for Monitor 2 to **1024 by 768 pixels**, and then click **OK**.

4 When prompted to confirm that you want to keep the new settings, click **Yes**.

52 **To move the taskbar to the external monitor**

1 Right-click on an empty area of the taskbar, and then click **Lock the Taskbar** to clear the selection.

2 Drag the taskbar to the external monitor.

53 **To create a .NET Passport account and link it to your Windows XP user account**

1 Click **Start**, click **Control Panel**, and then click **User Accounts**.

2 In the User Accounts window, click the **User Accounts** link.

3 In the **User Accounts** dialog box click the **Advanced** tab, and then click **.NET Passport Wizard**.

4 On the first page of the .NET Passport Wizard, click **Next**.

5 On the **Do you have an e-mail address** page, click **No, I would like to open an MSN Hotmail account**, and then click **Next**.

6 On the **Register with Hotmail and .NET Passport** page, click **Next**.

7 In the Get a .NET Passport window, fill in the registration information, read through the Hotmail Agreements section, and then click **I Agree**.

8 On the **Registration is Complete** page, click **Continue**.

9 On the **Associate Your .NET Passport** page, click **Next**.

10 In the **User Accounts** dialog box, click **OK**.

53 **To install the latest version of MSN Messenger**

1 Click **Start**, and then click **Internet Explorer**.

2 In the Address Bar of the Internet Explorer window, type http://messenger.msn.com.

3 On the **MSN Messenger** page, click **Download Now**.

4 In the **Registered MSN User** area of the **Download MSN Messenger** page, click **Go**.

5 On the **Get started with MSN Messenger** page, follow the instructions to complete the download.

56 **To sign into MSN Messenger, customize your name, select a personalized picture, and then add a contact**

1 Click **Start**, point to **All Programs**, and then click **MSN Messenger**.

2 In the MSN Messenger window, click the **Tools** menu, and then click **Options**.

3   In the **Type your name as you want others to see it** box, type the name that you want to appear in the MSN Messenger window.

4   In the **My Display Picture** area, click **Change Picture**.

5   In the **My Personal Picture** dialog box, in the list of images, click a picture that you want displayed, and then click **OK**.

6   In the **Options** dialog box, click **OK**.

7   In the MSN Messenger window, click the **Add a Contact** link at the bottom of the window.

8   In the **Add a Contact** dialog box, select the **Create a new contact by entering their e-mail address or sign-in name** option, and then click **Next**.

9   In the **Please type your contact's complete e-mail address** box, type the e-mail address of the contact you wish to add, and then click **Next**.

10 On the last page of the wizard, click **Finish**.

60 **To start a conversation with an online contact, send a file, and share an electronic whiteboard**

1   Double-click on the **MSN Messenger** icon in the notification area.

2   In the MSN Messenger window, double-click the name of an online contact with whom you want to start a conversation.

3   In the Conversation window, type your message, and then click **Send**.

4   To send an emoticon, click the **Select an emoticon** button above the text input area, choose one from the menu that appears, and then click **Send**.

5   To send a file to a contact, in the **I want to** area at the bottom of the MSN Messenger window, click the **Send a File or Photo** link.

6   In the **Send a File** dialog box, click the name of the contact with whom you want to share the file, and then click **OK**.

7   In the **Send a File** dialog box, browse to a file that you want to send, and then click **Open**.

8   To share a whiteboard with your contact, click the **Action** menu, click **Start Whiteboard**, and then type your message.

64 **To send a handwritten message to a contact by using your Tablet PC and MSN Messenger**

1   Double-click the **MSN Messenger** icon in the notification area.

2   In the MSN Messenger window, double-click the name of an online contact with whom you wish to start a conversation.

3 In the Conversation window, click the **Handwrite** tab.

4 Using the Tablet pen, handwrite your message, and then click **Send**.

65 **To use the new Tablet PC Input Panel to enter text in Notepad**

1 Tap **Start**, tap **All Programs**, tap **Accessories**, and then tap **Notepad**.

2 Tap where you want to insert text and keep the tip of the tablet pen close to the screen.

3 Tap the **Tablet PC Input Panel** icon.

4 In Input Panel, tap the **Writing Pad** button.

5 On the character pad, write a message.

6 To insert the text into the active Notepad document, tap **Insert**.

7 In Input Panel, tap the **On-Screen Keyboard** button.

8 Using the on-screen keyboard, type a message.

65 **To enter a Web site address in a Web browser by using the Tablet PC Input Panel**

1 Tap **Start**, and then tap **Internet Explorer**.

2 In the Internet Explorer window, tap the **Address Bar**.

3 Tap the **Tablet PC Input Panel** icon, and then tap the **Character Pad** button.

4 To expedite the entry of the Web site address, tap **http://**, and then tap **www**.

5 By tapping the characters in the character pad, write microsoft.

6 After Input Panel recognizes the word *microsoft* and inserts it in the Address Bar, tap **.com**, and then tap **Insert**.

7 To open the Web page, tap **Go**.

71 **To configure your computer to use offline files**

1 Click **Start**, click **Control Panel**, and then click **Appearance and Themes**.

2 In the Appearance and Themes window, click the **Folder Options** link.

3 In the **Folder Options** dialog box, click the **Offline Files** tab.

4 Select the **Enable Offline Files** and **Create an Offline Files shortcut on the desktop** check boxes, and then click **OK**.

71 **To specify the files and folders that you want to access offline**

1 Click **Start**, and then click **My Network Places**.

2 Right-click the network folder that you want to make available offline, and then click **Make Available Offline**.

71 To access offline files

- On the desktop, double-click the **Shortcut To Offline Files** icon.

74 To use Internet Explorer to make a Web page available offline

1. Click **Start**, and then click **Internet Explorer**.
2. In the Address Bar of the Internet Explorer window, type an address you frequently visit, and then click **Go**.
3. Click the **Favorites** menu, and then click **Add To Favorites**.
4. In the **Add Favorite** dialog box, select the **Make available offline** check box.
5. To start the initial synchronization process, click **OK**.
6. In the Internet Explorer window, click the **Home** button.
7. Click the **File** menu, and then click **Work Offline**.

74 To verify that you can view the contents of the Web page while offline

- Click the **Favorites** menu, and then click the name of the Web page.

74 To find out what happens when you try connecting to a Web page that you have not made available offline

1. In the **Address Bar**, type www.microsoft.com, and then click **Go**.
2. To re-establish your Internet connection, click **Connect**.

78 To manually turn off extended desktop mode before undocking

1. Right-click the desktop, and then click **Properties**.
2. In the **Display Properties** dialog box, click the **Settings** tab.
3. On the **Settings** tab, clear the **Extend my Windows desktop to this monitor** check box, and then click **OK**.

Chapter 5 Using Your Mobile PC in Meetings

Page 85 To configure your mobile PC to use the extended desktop mode

1. Right-click the desktop, and then click **Properties**.
2. In the **Display Properties** dialog box, click the **Settings** tab.
3. Click the visual representation of Monitor 2, select the **Extend my Windows desktop onto this monitor** check box, and then click **OK**.
4. If an image of your desktop background is showing on the second monitor's screen while your mobile PC screen continues to show not only your desktop background, but also your taskbar, any open programs, icons, and so on, click **Yes**.

86 **To change the position of Monitor 2 to better reflect its physical position**

1   Right-click the desktop, and then click **Properties**.

2   In the **Display Properties** dialog box, click the **Settings** tab.

3   Drag the graphical representation of Monitor 2 to the left of Monitor 1, and then click **OK**.

87 **To move the Microsoft Internet Explorer program to the other monitor**

1   Click **Start**, and then click **Internet Explorer**.

2   Drag the Internet Explorer window to the second monitor.

87 **To make the Internet Explorer window fill the second screen**

●   Click the **Maximize** button on the title bar of the window.

87 **To stop using extended desktop mode**

1   Right-click the desktop, click **Properties**, and then in the **Display Properties** dialog box, click the **Settings** tab.

2   On the **Settings** tab, clear the **Extend my Windows desktop onto this monitor** check box, and then click **OK**.

88 **To show a presentation using the PowerPoint Presenter View**

1   Click **Start**, point to **All Programs**, point to **Microsoft Office**, and then click **Microsoft PowerPoint**.

2   On the **Slide Show** menu, click **Set Up Show**.

3   In the **Set Up Show** dialog box, select the **Show Presenter View** check box, and then click **OK**.

4   On the **File** menu, click **Open**.

5   In the **Name** box of the **Open** dialog box, browse to your presentation.

91 **To use a USB flash drive to quickly and reliably move data between computers**

1   Plug the USB flash drive into an available USB port.

2   Click **Start**, and then click **My Computer**.

3   In the **My Computer** folder, double-click the **USB Drive** icon to display a list of the files stored on the drive.

Use the files like you would with files stored on any other storage device.

92 To check the availability of infrared on your computer

1 Click **Start**, right-click **My Computer**, and then click **Properties**.

2 In the **Systems Properties** dialog box, click the **Hardware** tab, and then click **Device Manager**.

3 In the Device Manager window, scroll down the list until you locate the **Infrared devices** section.

92 To send files to another computer by using infrared data transmission

1 Place the two computers within 3 feet of each other, and make sure that the infrared ports are facing each other.

2 After the connection between the computers has been established, in the notification area, double-click the **Wireless Link** icon.

3 In the **Wireless Link** dialog box, select the files you want to share, and then click **Send**.

4 When a message box appears on the second PC notifying you that files have been sent and are available for download, click **Yes** to start the file transfer process.

5 To terminate the connection, move the PCs so that the infrared ports do not point at each other.

95 To create an ad hoc wireless network when you are using a USB flash drive

1 Click **Start**, click **Control Panel**, and then click **Network and Internet Connections**.

2 In the Network and Internet Connections window, click **Network Connections**.

3 In the Network Connections window, right-click the **Wireless Network Connection** icon, and then click **View Available Wireless Network**.

4 In the **Network Tasks** area of the **Wireless Network Connection** dialog box, click the **Set up a wireless network** link.

5 On the first page of the Wireless Network Setup Wizard, click **Next**.

6 On the **Choose a key for your wireless network** page, enter a name for the network, and click **Next**.

7 On the **Choose a method for setting up your wireless network** page, click **Next**.

8 Insert the USB flash drive into the USB port of your computer, and then on the **Save settings to your flash drive** page, click **Next**.

9 Unplug the USB flash drive and plug it into the computer you want to add to your network.

10 In the **What do you want Windows to do?** area, click **Wireless Network Setup Wizard**, and then click **OK**.

11 When prompted to confirm the addition of the computer to the new ad hoc wireless network, click **OK**.

95 **To share a folder with other network users**

1 Click **Start**, and then click **My Documents**.

2 In the My Documents window, browse to the folder you want to share.

3 On the **File and Folder Tasks** menu, click **Share This Folder**.

4 In the **My Shared Files Properties** dialog box, click the **Sharing** tab, click the **Share This Folder** option, and then click **OK**.

100 **To modify power options to ensure that your computer screen never turns off**

1 Click **Start**, click **Control Panel**, and then click **Performance and Maintenance**.

2 In the Performance and Maintenance window, click **Power Options**.

3 On the **Power Scheme**s tab of the **Power Options Properties** dialog box, click the **Power schemes** arrow, and then click **Presentation** in the drop-down list.

4 To apply and use the **Presentation** power scheme, click **OK**.

5 When you have finished the presentation, in the notification area, right-click the battery meter icon, and then click **Adjust Power Options**.

6 On the **Power Schemes** tab of the **Power Options Properties** dialog box, click the **Power schemes** arrow and click **Portable/Laptop** in the list.

102 **To adjust the screen brightness setting to lessen power consumption on a Tablet PC**

1 In the notification area, double-tap the **Change tablet and pen settings** icon.

2 In the **Tablet and Pen Settings** dialog box, click the **Display** tab.

3 In the **Screen Brightness** area, click the down arrow to the right of the **Settings for** button, and then click **Powered by batteries**.

4 Move the **Brightness** slider to the left to dim the screen and lessen the power on the battery, and then click **OK**.

103 **To take notes on your Tablet PC by using Microsoft Office OneNote 2003 Service Pack 1 (SP1)**

1 Tap **Start**, tap **All Programs**, tap **Microsoft Office**, and then tap **Microsoft OneNote 2003**.

2 In the **Section Tabs** area, tap the **Meetings** tab.

3 On the right side of the note page, tap the **New Page** icon to create a page.

4   In the **Title** box at the top of the page, using your Tablet PC pen, write a title for your note, and then in the body of the page, write your note.

103   **To open an existing note page**

●   In OneNote, browse to the folder containing the note page, and then tap the note page.

103   **To add a page so that you can add more notes**

●   In the lower-right corner of the page, tap the **Page Down** icon.

103   **To flag part of a note as an important issue to follow up on**

●   Select the text you want to flag, tap the **Note Flag** arrow, and then tap **Important** in the menu.

103   **To convert an action item into a task that you can track using Outlook**

1   Select the item you want to track, and then, on the **Format** menu, tap **Note Flags**.

2   Tap **Create Outlook Task**, and then click the **Save and Close** button.

103   **To select an area of screen to insert into your notes**

1   Click the **Insert** menu, and then click **Screen Clipping**.

2   Holding down the tablet pen button, drag to select the area of the screen that you wish to capture and to include in your note.

Chapter 6   **Using Your Mobile PC at Home**

Page 112   **To provide a description for your mobile PC and change its name**

1   Click **Start**, right-click **My Computer**, and then click **Properties**.

2   In the **System Properties** dialog box, click the **Computer Name** tab.

3   In the **Computer description** box, type the name you want to give to your computer.

4   To modify the computer name, click **Change**.

5   In the **Computer Name Changes** dialog box, type a new name.

6   To close the open dialog boxes and not apply the changes, click **Cancel** twice.

113   **To set up a wireless home network**

1   Click **Start**, click **Control Panel**, and then click **Network and Internet Connections**.

2   In the **Network and Internet Connections** window, click **Set up a wireless network for a home or small office**.

3 On the wizard's first page, click **Next**.

4 In the **Network name (SSID)** box, type the name of your network, make sure that the **Automatically assign a network key (recommended)** option is selected, and then click **Next**.

5 On the **How do you want to setup your network?** page, select the **Use a USB flash drive** option, and then click **Next**.

6 Plug your USB flash drive into your USB port, click the USB flash drive in the **Flash drive** drop-down list, and then click **Next**.

7 Remove the USB flash drive from your mobile PC's USB port, and then plug it into your wireless access point.

8 Plug in the USB flash drive in each of the computers you want to join the home network.

9 When you are done, plug the USB flash drive back into the mobile PC you started the process on, and then click **Next**.

10 Click **Finish**.

116 **To make a printer available to all of the computers connected to your home network**

1 Click **Start**, and then click **Printers and Faxes**.

2 In the Printers and Faxes window, right-click the icon for the printer that you want to share, and then click **Sharing**.

3 On the **Sharing** tab of the printer **Properties** dialog box, select the **Share this printer** option.

4 In the **Share name** box, type the name that you want to give your printer network, and then click **OK**.

116 **To stop sharing a network printer**

1 Click **Start**, and then click **Printers and Faxes**.

2 In the Printers and Faxes window, right-click the icon for the printer that you want to discontinue sharing, and then click **Sharing**.

3 On the **Sharing** tab of the **Properties** dialog box, select the **Don't share this printer** option, and then click **OK**.

118 **To share a folder**

1 Click **Start**, and then click **My Documents**.

2 In the My Documents window, browse to the folder on which you want to set access permissions, right-click the folder, and then click **Sharing and Security**.

3   In the folder **Properties** dialog box on the **Sharing** tab, select the **Share this folder** option.

4   To set user permissions for the folder, in the **Permissions for** dialog box in the **Allow** column, select the **Change** check box.

5   To share the folder with other users on your network, click **OK** twice.

6   On a different computer connected to the network, click **Start**, and then click **My Computer** to confirm that the folder is shared over the network.

7   In the My Computer window in the **Other Places** area, click **My Network Places**.

118   **To view the contents of a shared folder**

●   Locate the shared folder, and then double-click it.

118   **To stop sharing a network folder**

1   Click **Start**, and then click **My Documents**.

2   In the My Documents window, locate the shared folder, right-click it, and then click **Sharing and Security**.

3   In the **Properties** dialog box, on the **Sharing** tab, select the **Do not share this folder** option, and then click **OK**.

121   **To transfer files and folders from one computer to another by using the Files and Settings Transfer Wizard**

1   Click **Start**, point to **Programs**, point to **Accessories**, point to **System Tools**, and then click **Files and Settings Transfer Wizard**.

2   On the first page of the Files and Settings Transfer Wizard, click **Next**.

3   On the **Which computer is this?** page, select the **Old Computer** option, and then click **Next**.

4   On the "Select a transfer method" page, select the **Home or small office network** option, and then click **Next**.

5   Determine exactly what you want transferred (settings, files or both), browse to the information that you want to transfer, and then double-click it.

6   Go to the other computer that you want to transfer the information to and repeat the process.

7   On the **Which computer is this?** page, select the **New Computer** option, and then click **Next**.

8   When you're done, click **Finish**.

122 **To create a VPN connection to a corporate network**

1 Click **Start**, click **Control Panel**, and then click **Network and Internet Connections**.

2 In the Network and Internet Connections window, click **Create a connection to the network at your workplace**.

3 On the **Network Connection** page, select the **Virtual Private Network connection** option, and then click **Next**.

4 On the **Connection Name** page in the **Company** box, type the name of your company, and then click **Next**.

5 On the **Public Network** page, select the **Do not dial the initial connection** option, and then click **Next**.

6 On the **VPN Server Selection** page, type the host name or IP address for your company's remote access server, and then click **Next**.

7 If you have a smart card, on the **Smart Cards** page, make sure that the **Do not use my smart card** option is selected, and then click **Next**.

8 On the **Connection Availability** page, make sure that the **My use only** option is selected, and then click **Next**.

9 On the **Completing the New Connection Wizard** page, click **Finish**.

122 **To test the newly created VPN connection**

1 In the Network and Internet Connections window, click **Network Connections**.

2 In the Network Connections window, double-click the icon representing the connection you just created.

3 In the dialog box that appears, type your user name and password, and then click **Connect**.

122 **To close the VPN connection**

● Right-click the network icon in the notification area, and then click **Disconnect**.

122 **To delete the VPN connection**

1 In the Network Connections window, right-click the icon representing the VPN connection that you want to delete, and then click **Delete**.

2 When prompted to confirm the deletion, click **Yes**.

126 **To enable your work computer to be accessed through Remote Desktop**

1 Click **Start**, click **Control Panel**, and then click **Performance and Maintenance**.

2 In the Performance and Maintenance window, click **System**.

3   In the **System Properties** dialog box, click the **Remote** tab.

4   In the **Remote Desktop** area, select the **Allow users to connect remotely to this computer** check box, and then click **OK**.

126   **To start a Remote Desktop session**

1   Click **Start**, point to **All Programs**, point to **Accessories**, point to **Communications**, and then click **Remote Desktop Connection**.

2   In the **Remote Desktop Connection** dialog box, type the name or the IP address of your work computer.

126   **To end a Remote Desktop session**

●   Click the **Close** button on the Remote Desktop window title bar.

127   **To train your Tablet PC to recognize your voice**

1   Tap the **Tablet PC Input Panel** icon.

2   On the right side of the Tablet PC Input Panel, tap the **Tools and Options** button, and then tap **Speech**.

3   In the **Speech Recognition Enrollment** dialog box, tap **Next**.

4   On the **Microphone Wizard Welcome** page, follow the instructions to adjust your microphone, and then click **Next**.

5   Read aloud the paragraphs on the page.

6   Click **Next**.

127   **To test the speech functionality**

1   Tap **Start**, tap **All Programs**, tap **Accessories**, and then tap **WordPad**.

2   Press and hold the **Dictation** button in the Table PC Input Panel and then say This is a test.

3   When you're finished speaking, release the **Dictation** button.

Chapter 7   **At Home: Playing and Sharing Digital Media**

Page 132   **To play music in Windows Media Player**

1   Click **Start**, point to **All Programs**, and then click **Windows Media Player**.

2   Open the optical drive tray on your mobile PC and insert a music CD.

3   Click the **Now Playing** down arrow, and then click **CD Drive**.

141 **To use Windows Media Player to listen to a radio station**

1 Click **Start**, and then click **Windows Media Player**.

2 On the Windows Media Player taskbar, click the **Radio** tab.

3 To open the current list of international radio stations, click the icon to the left of **International**.

4 Select a radio station, and then click the **Play** icon.

143 **To use Windows Media Player 10 to play a DVD on your mobile PC**

1 Insert the DVD into the DVD drive of your mobile PC.

2 In the **Autoplay** dialog box, click **Play DVD using Windows Media Player**.

144 **To copy a music album to a portable device**

1 Click **Start**, and then click **Windows Media Player**.

2 Plug your portable device into your mobile PC.

3 In the **Device Setup** dialog box, select the **Automatic** option, and then click **Finish**.

4 When the synchronization is complete, unplug your device, and then click the **Close** button.

146 **To transfer pictures from your digital camera to your mobile PC**

1 Connect your digital camera to your mobile PC.

2 Click **Microsoft Scanner and Camera Wizard**, and then click **OK**.

3 On the first page of the Microsoft Scanner and Camera Wizard, click **Next**.

4 On the **Choose Pictures to Copy** page, select the check boxes corresponding to the pictures that you want to copy to your mobile PC, and then click **Next**.

5 On the **Picture Name and Destination** page, type a name in the **Type a name for this group of pictures** box, and then click **Next**.

6 On the **Other Options** page, select the **Nothing. I'm finished working with these pictures** option, and then click **Next**.

7 Click **Finish**.

146 **To view your pictures on your computer**

1 Click **Start**, and then click **My Pictures**.

2 In the My Pictures window, double-click the folder that you created in step 5 of the previous procedure.

3 To view the next picture in the list, click the **Next Image** button.

4 In the **Picture Tasks** area, click **View as a slide show**.

149 **To publish your pictures to a Web site**

1 Start the Microsoft Scanner and Camera Wizard, and then click **Next**.

2 On the **Choose Pictures to Copy** page, select the check boxes corresponding to the pictures that you want to copy to your mobile PC, and then click **Next**.

3 On the **Picture Name and Destination** page, type a name in the **Type a name or this group of pictures** box, and then click **Next**.

4 On the **Other Options** page, select the **Publish these pictures to a Web site** option.

5 On the **Change Your File Selection** page, select the list of pictures that you want to share, and then click **Next**.

6 On the **Where do you want to publish these files?** page, select the Web site provider you want to use to share your pictures.

Chapter 8 **Traveling with Your Mobile PC**

Page 156 **To connect to a public wireless network**

1 Click **Start**, click **Control Panel**, and then click **Network and Internet Connections**.

2 In the Network and Internet Connections window, click **Network Connections**.

3 In the Network Connections window, click the **Wireless Network Connection** icon.

4 In the **Network Tasks** area, click **View available wireless networks**.

5 In the Wireless Network Connection window, click **Find a wireless network location** under **Related Tasks**.

6 Complete the fields to search for a wireless public Internet service provider (ISP) in a specific location.

159 **To turn off wireless networking on your mobile PC**

1 Click **Start**, click **Control Panel**, and then click **Network and Internet Connections**.

2 In the Network and Internet Connections window, click **Network Connections**.

3 In the Network Connections window, right click the **Wireless Network Connection** icon, and then click **Disable**.

162 **To explore one of the built-in power schemes and then create a custom one**

1 Click **Start**, click **Control Panel**, and then click **Performance and Maintenance**.

2 In the Performance and Maintenance window, click **Power Options**.

3   In the **Power Options Properties** dialog box, click the **Power scheme** down arrow, and then click **Max Battery**.

4   To create a custom power scheme based on this built-in scheme, in the **Running on batteries** area, click the **Turn off monitor** down arrow, and then from the list, click **3 minutes**.

5   Click the **Turn off hard disk** down arrow, and then in the list, click **5 minutes**.

6   To save these settings as a new power scheme, click **Save As**.

7   In the **Save Scheme** dialog box, type Transit, and then click **OK**.

8   To select another built-in power scheme, click the **Power scheme** down arrow, and then click **Portable/Laptop**.

9   To apply the currently selected power scheme, click **OK**.

Chapter 9   Maintaining and Protecting Your Mobile PC

Page 167   **To run Disk Cleanup on your mobile PC**

1   Click **Start**, point to **All Programs**, point to **Accessories**, point to **System Tools**, and then click **Disk Cleanup**.

2   In the **Disk Cleanup for** dialog box, scroll through the content of the **Files to delete** list.

3   Clear the check boxes in front of files that you don't want to delete, and then click **OK**.

4   When prompted to confirm that you want to delete the specified files, click **Yes**.

169   **To run the Disk Defragmenter utility**

1   Click **Start**, point to **All Programs**, point to **Accessories**, point to **System Tools**, and then click **Disk Defragmenter**.

2   In the **Disk Defragmenter** dialog box, click the drives that you want to defragment, and then click the **Analyze** button.

3   If the result of the analysis advises you to defragment the drive, click the **Defragment** button.

4   To display detailed information about the defragmented disk or partition, click **View Report**.

171   **To run the Check Disk utility**

1   Click **Start**, and then click **My Computer**.

2   In the My Computer window, right-click the hard disk you want to search for bad sectors, and then click **Properties**.

3 In the dialog box that appears, click the **Tools** tab.

4 Click the **Check Now** button.

5 In the **Check Disk** dialog box, select the **Scan for and attempt recovery of bad sectors** check box, and then click **Start**.

173 **To back up the contents of your My Documents and Favorites folders, as well as your desktop settings and any saved cookies**

1 Click **Start**, point to **All Programs**, point to **Accessories**, point to **System Tools**, and then click **Backup**.

2 On the first page of the Backup or Restore Wizard, click **Next**.

3 On the **Backup or Restore** page, make sure that the **Back up files and settings** option is selected, and then click **Next**.

4 On the **What to Back Up** page, make sure that the **My documents and settings** option is selected and then click **Next**.

5 On the **Backup Type, Destination, and Name** page, click the **Browse** button.

6 In the **Save As** dialog box, click the **Save in** down arrow, and then click **Desktop**.

7 To name the backup file, click in the **File name** box, type the name you want to give the file, and then click **Save**.

8 On the **Backup Type, Destination, and Name** page, click **Next**.

9 To back up the selected files and settings, click **Finish**.

10 To close the **Backup Progress** dialog box, click **Close**.

173 **To restore backed up files**

1 Click **Start**, point to **All Programs**, point to **Accessories**, point to **System Tools**, and then click **Backup**.

2 On the first page of the Backup or Restore Wizard, click **Next**.

3 On the **Backup or Restore** page, select the **Restore files and settings** option, and then click **Next**.

4 On the **What to Restore** page, click the plus sign to the right of the **File** icon, click the plus sign to the right of the file name, select the check box of the drive you want to restore, and then click **Next**.

5 To restore the backed up files and settings, click **Finish**.

176 **To restore the system to a previous state**

1 Click **Start**, point to **All Programs**, point to **Accessories**, point to **System Tools**, and then click **System Restore**.

2   Click **Next**.

3   On the calendar, select a date in bold for the restore point.

4   Click **Next** twice.

178   **To adjust the security settings used by Internet Explorer for different content zones**

1   Click **Start**, and then click **Internet Explorer**.

2   In Internet Explorer, click the **Tools** menu, and then click **Internet Options**.

3   In the **Internet Options** dialog box, click the **Security** tab.

4   In the **Select a Web content zone to specify its security settings** area, click **Internet**.

5   In the **Security level for this zone** area, click **Default Level**.

6   To ensure safe and functional Web surfing while still preventing unsigned ActiveX controls from downloading, move the slide up to **Medium** and then click **OK**.

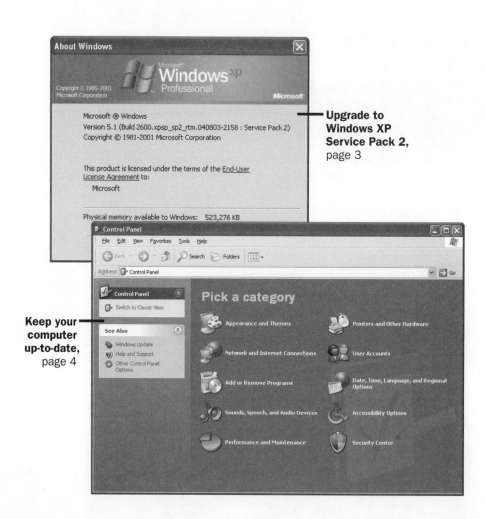

Upgrade to
**Windows XP
Service Pack 2,**
page 3

**Keep your
computer
up-to-date,**
page 4

Chapter 1 at a Glance

1 Running Microsoft Windows XP on a Mobile PC

In this chapter you will learn to:

✔ Choose a Windows XP edition for your mobile PC.

✔ Understand Windows XP Service Pack 2.

✔ Upgrade to Windows XP Service Pack 2.

✔ Keep your computer up-to-date.

✔ Understand mobile PC usage scenarios.

Over the past few years, mobile PC sales have seen a significant and consistent upward trend. More and more people are choosing to buy a laptop or a Tablet PC rather than a traditional desktop PC. This shift is happening for several reasons:

■ Mobile PCs are becoming more affordable.

■ Mobile PCs are getting smaller and lighter.

■ Mobile PC battery life is getting longer.

■ Mobile PCs are becoming as powerful as their desktop counterparts.

Microsoft Windows XP offers a multitude of features that make it even easier to use a mobile PC. In 2002, Microsoft introduced Windows XP Tablet PC Edition, specifically for the next generation of mobile PCs.

If you have a mobile PC or are considering buying one, you have probably thought about the different ways you could use it at home, at work, or while on the go. Throughout this book, you will learn how to take full advantage of Windows XP features to go truly mobile with your laptop or Tablet PC. In this chapter, you will learn about the different versions of Windows XP that are available for your mobile PC. You will also learn about Windows XP Service Pack 2 (SP2) and how to install it. This chapter also introduces you to some of the key features on your mobile PC that make it an indispensable addition to your busy life.

See Also Do you need only a quick refresher on the topics in this chapter? See the Quick Reference entries on page xix.

Important   Throughout this book, we refer to laptops and Tablet PCs by the generic term of *mobile PCs*. Most of the information in the book is equally applicable to laptops and Tablet PCs. Any content specific to the Tablet PCs is identified by the icon shown in the margin.

Choosing a Windows XP Edition for Your Mobile PC

There are four versions of Windows XP that could be installed on your mobile PC:

- *Windows XP Home Edition.*   This basic version is designed for home computers. It does not allow the computer to connect to a corporate network and lacks a couple of other administrative features that the other versions of Windows XP have. If you purchased your laptop from a retailer, you are probably running Windows XP Home Edition.

- *Windows XP Professional.*   This version is designed primarily for business use (although it can be used at home too) and can connect to a corporate network. If your laptop was issued to you by your company or organization, it probably came with Windows XP Professional.

- *Windows XP Tablet PC Edition.*   This version is only available on Tablet PCs, the next generation of mobile PCs. It allows you to use a special pen to write notes and enter text directly on the Tablet PC screen.

- *Windows XP Media Center Edition.*   This version can be used to record TV shows, play music, view photos, and watch shows on your television set. It also comes with a remote control so that you can control your computer while sitting on your couch. Windows XP Media Center Edition is available on some laptops models.

Understanding Windows XP Service Pack 2

In August 2004, Microsoft released a free update to Windows XP that includes a number of new enhancements that make Windows XP an even better operating system for mobile PCs. These enhancements include:

- *Security improvements.*   One of the main focuses of SP2 is security. The following improvements make Windows XP a more secure operating system:

  - Windows Security Center is a central place for you to view your security settings and learn more about how to improve the security of your computer with Windows Firewall, Automatic Updates, and antivirus software.

  - Windows Firewall is now automatically enabled and helps protect your computer against viruses and other security threats, such as intruders who might try to access your computer over the Internet.

■ Automatic Updates ensures that your computer remains up-to-date with the latest security patches.

■ Tighter control of downloaded files prevents harmful content from reaching your computer.

■ *Pop-up blocker.* You can use Internet Explorer to stop most pop-up windows, giving you more control over your Web browsing experience.

■ *Wireless networking improvements.* SP2 makes it easier to create and connect to wireless networks at home or work.

■ *Windows XP Tablet PC Edition 2005.* If you have a Tablet PC, SP2 includes an updated version of Windows XP Tablet PC Edition, which offers better hand-writing recognition and an improved Tablet PC Input Panel.

See Also For more information about Windows XP Service Pack 2, visit *www.microsoft.com /windowsxp/sp2/*.

Upgrading to Windows XP Service Pack 2

If your computer isn't already running Windows XP SP2, you can upgrade it to take advantage of all of the enhancements and improvements highlighted in the previous section. All of the exercises presented in this book require Windows XP SP2.

In this exercise, you will determine what version of Windows XP you are running and download Service Pack 2 if necessary.

BE SURE TO log in as an administrator and have an active Internet connection before beginning this exercise.

1 Click **Start**, and then click **My Computer**.

2 In the My Computer window, click **Help**, and then click **About Windows**.

The second line of text in the About Windows dialog box identifies the version of Windows that you are running. If the words *Service Pack 2* do not appear at the end of the line (as shown in the example on the next page), follow the remaining steps to install SP2.

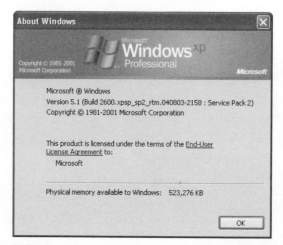

3 To close the **About Windows** dialog box, click **OK**.

Close

4 Click the **Close** button.

Important If you have SP2 installed, you can skip the remaining steps.

5 To install SP2, click **Start**, point to **All Programs**, and then click **Windows Update**.

6 On the Windows Update home page, click the **Express Installation** link.

7 Review the list of high priority updates, and then click **Install**.

The Installing Updates dialog box tracks the installation progress.

Tip If you're connecting to the Internet by means of a dial-up connection, downloading SP2 might not be feasible because it will take a long time to download. You can order a free SP2 installation CD from *www.microsoft.com/athome/security /protect/cd/confirm.aspx*.

8 When prompted to accept the license agreement, read the agreement, and then, if you accept the agreement conditions, click **Yes**.

9 When prompted to restart your computer, click **Restart Now**.

Keeping Your Computer Up-to-Date

When you install SP2, the Automatic Updates feature is turned on by default. Whenever you are connected to the Internet, the Automatic Updates feature downloads the latest updates; you can configure it to automatically install the downloaded updates for you.

In this exercise, you will specify when you want to install updates.

BE SURE TO log in as an administrator before beginning this exercise.

1   Click **Start**, and then click **Control Panel**.

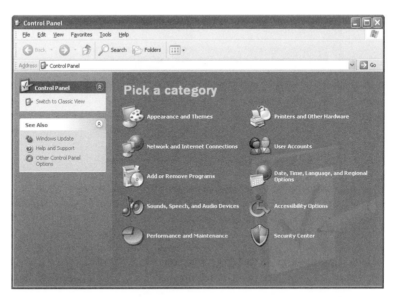

2   In Control Panel in the **Pick a category** area, click **Security Center**.

You can control the various security settings for your computer from the Security Center window. It also includes links to other security information on the Internet.

3 In the Windows Security Center window in the **Manage security settings for** area, click **Automatic Updates**.

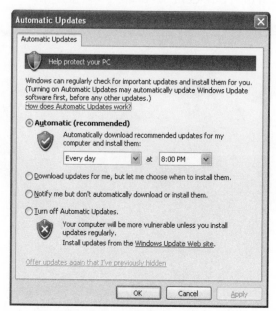

4 In the **Automatic Updates** dialog box, make sure that the **Automatic (recommended)** option is selected and specify the time and frequency for installation of the updates you want to receive.

Important Be sure to pick a time when the computer is usually turned on.

5 To apply the changes, click **OK**.

6 Click the **Close** button.

Close

CLOSE Control Panel.

Important Windows installs any downloaded updates before shutting down your computer.

Understanding Mobile PC Usage Scenarios

Throughout the remainder of this book, you will learn how to use your mobile PC in a variety of different settings and for various purposes. Scenarios are a useful way to describe situations and environments in which a mobile PC can be used. The purpose of the scenarios is to show how you can take advantage of the features presented in Windows XP to complete tasks that you perform regularly or that you want your mobile PC to do. The scenarios presented in this book are only examples, but in no way are they limiting. For example, Chapter 4, "Using Your Mobile PC at Your Desk," describes using MSN Messenger while you are in the office, but the scenario could equally be used in a meeting or at home. When reading through the rest of the book, try to think about how you could apply the exercises in other ways.

Using Your Mobile PC in the Office

Using your mobile PC as part of your job is probably the most common scenario. Companies have realized the increased productivity that comes with providing employees with a mobile PC. In this book, two different office scenarios are covered:

■ *At your desk.* If you have an office-bound job, you probably spend most of your time at your desk. In that case, your mobile PC is likely to be used for reading and sending e-mail messages, writing documents and spreadsheets, and using any other programs specific to your company. Chapter 4, "Using Your Mobile PC at Your Desk," introduces the use of a docking station to expand the hardware capabilities of your mobile PC so that you can use a larger keyboard, an external mouse, and a larger monitor.

■ *In meetings.* It is gradually becoming more common and culturally accepted for people to take their mobile PCs to meetings, either to present and share information with other people or to take notes. The Tablet PC provides great ways to use a mobile PC to take notes. Chapter 5, "Using Your Mobile PC in Meetings," covers all of this and more.

Using Your Mobile PC at Home

If your organization provides a mobile PC for your use, you will probably want to bring it home at some point to get some work done. If you have purchased your mobile PC for personal use, it might be the sole computer in the house, or you might have purchased it as an additional computer for a family member to supplement the other desktop PCs in the house.

If there are several computers in your house, be sure to consider the huge benefits that a home network would provide. With a home network, you can share information between your mobile PC and the other computers in the house, use your mobile PC to access the Internet from home—with a wireless network, you can do this without having to leave the comfort of your couch—and use your home printer. Chapter 6, "Using Your Mobile PC at Home," covers how to make of the most out of adding your mobile PC to a home network.

Your mobile PC also makes a great entertainment device. You might bring your mobile PC home to surf the Web, play games, listen to music, watch a DVD, or manage pictures taken with your digital camera. Chapter 7, "At Home: Playing and Sharing Digital Media," introduces you to some of the ways in which you can use your mobile PC for entertainment.

Using Your Mobile PC While Traveling

One of the true benefits of a mobile PC is your ability to take it with you while on the go. Whether you are on a business trip, on a family vacation, or running errands around town, the mobile PC can be an invaluable companion. You can use a wireless network in a coffee shop or in a hotel to connect to the Internet and find out where to find the best local restaurants. You can also sit back on a long flight and watch a DVD of your choice. Chapter 3, "Introduction to Networking," covers how to connect your mobile PC to a wireless network and Chapter 8, "Traveling with Your Mobile PC," provides tips on how to use your mobile PC while traveling.

Using Your Mobile PC as a Student

Although there is no section of the book dedicated to students using a mobile PC, all of the information described in the scenarios above is equally applicable. Students can use a mobile PC in the same ways the office and home scenarios describe. They can also use a mobile PC to take notes in college lectures, work at home on homework assignments, and enjoy the various entertainment options, such as playing digital music or watching a DVD in their dorm room.

Key Points

■ Several different versions of Windows XP exist for use on your mobile PC.

■ Windows XP Service Pack 2 is a free update to Windows XP that introduces several new security features and includes Windows XP Tablet PC Edition 2005.

■ You can use Automatic Updates to ensure that your computer is always up to date with the latest critical updates.

■ You can use your mobile PC in a variety of places and situations, including in the office, at home, and while traveling.

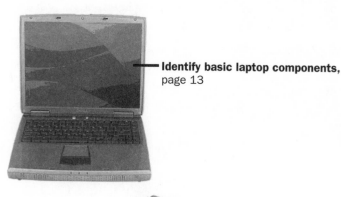

Identify basic laptop components,
page 13

Understand docking
stations and port replicators,
page 18

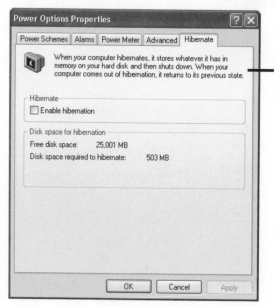

Effectively manage
your battery power,
page 27

Chapter 2 at a Glance

2 Getting to Know Your Mobile PC Hardware

In this chapter you will learn to:

✔ Identify basic laptop components.

✔ Identify laptop ports and jacks.

✔ Understand storage devices.

✔ Understand PC cards.

✔ Understand docking stations and port replicators.

✔ Work on a Tablet PC.

✔ Effectively manage your battery power.

All computers have a similar set of hardware components that you might already be familiar with. These components include a display screen, a keyboard, one or more hard drives, memory, and various ports and sockets. In addition to these common items, laptops offer a few unique components, such as a battery. When using a laptop, it is useful to be able to identify and understand the various components.

In this chapter you will learn to identify your laptop's basic components and its various ports and sockets. You will also learn about the different types of storage devices that come with laptops and learn how to use PC Cards. You will learn about the difference between docking stations and port replicators, other devices you can connect to your mobile PC, how to use a Tablet PC, and how to effectively manage your mobile PC's battery power.

See Also   Do you need only a quick refresher on the topics in this chapter? See the Quick Reference entries on pages xix–xx.

Important   Before you can use the practice files in this chapter, you need to install them from the book's companion CD to their default location. See "Using the Book's CD-ROM" on page xiii for more information.

Identifying Basic Laptop Components

Although every laptop is different, certain basic components do not vary. This section introduces the major components of a laptop and where they can usually be found.

When you open the lid of a laptop, you see the screen, the keyboard, and either a *touch pad* or a *track pointer-style* mouse, which controls the pointer.

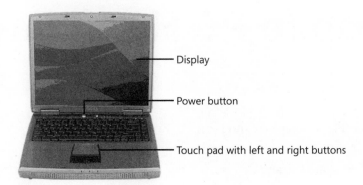

— Display

— Power button

— Touch pad with left and right buttons

Tip Touch pads and track pointer-style mice can be a little awkward to use and might require some practice. If you prefer, you can attach and use an external mouse.

The position of the power button varies. Some laptop designs have the power button near the keyboard or other hardware buttons (such as the volume and music playback control), while other laptops have the power button on the side of the computer.

Troubleshooting If your laptop stops responding and you're unable to shut it down by clicking **Start**, and then clicking **Shut Down**, try holding down the power button for 3 to 4 seconds to shut off the power to the computer.

The laptop's screen is a *liquid crystal display (LCD)* with a backlight to ensure that you can see the screen easily in different environments. Laptop screens vary in size and shape, depending on the manufacturer and model.

Improving Text Display by Using ClearType

Laptop screens are generally bright and easy to read, but the clarity of the text can be substandard (especially compared to desktop computer monitors). Microsoft ClearType, a component of Microsoft Windows XP, improves the way that text displays on an LCD screen and makes it much easier to read. On some laptops, ClearType is turned on by default.

To view your ClearType settings and turn on ClearType:

1 Click **Start**, click **Control Panel**, and then click **Appearance and Themes**.

2 In the **Appearance and Themes** window, click **Display**.

3 In the **Display Properties** dialog box, click the **Appearance** tab, and then click the **Effects** button.

4   In the **Effects** dialog box, select the **Use the following method to smooth edges of screen fonts** check box, click **ClearType** in the drop-down list, and then click **OK**.

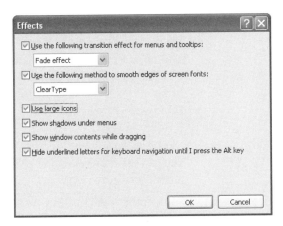

5   In the **Display Properties** dialog box, click **OK**.

Every laptop comes with a battery. The battery compartment is usually located on the bottom of the laptop. Some battery compartments are held closed by a small latch and can be opened by unclipping or sliding out the latch; others are screwed closed. You can purchase a second or more powerful battery to extend the time you can use your laptop without recharging it.

Theft of mobile PCs is an unfortunate fact of life. If you're concerned about your laptop getting stolen, you can use a special security cable that you affix to something immovable and then insert into the security port on your mobile PC. The security port is a small hole roughly 1/4 inch by 1/8 inch on the bezel of the mobile PC, usually on the back left or back right corner. It often has a padlock icon next to it. Security cables are available from most computer accessory retailers.

Identifying Laptop Ports and Jacks

When you look at the sides and back of your laptop, you find a range of ports and jacks. The exact combination and location depend on the laptop brand and model. The table on the next page describes the various ports and jacks you might find on your laptop.

Ports and jacks	Description and purpose	For more information, see
USB ports	Your laptop likely has one or more USB ports to which you can connect devices. Common USB devices include: External keyboards and mice Digital cameras Digital audio players You can use more than one USB port at the same time.	
Dedicated keyboard and mouse ports — Typical mouse plug Keyboard and mouse socket Typical keyboard plug	Your laptop might include dedicated ports for an external keyboard and mouse. External keyboards and mice are particularly convenient if you are using your laptop for an extended period of time at a desk.	Chapters 3 and 6
Network ports — Ethernet cable — Ethernet port	Most laptops have an Ethernet network port. With this port, you can connect your laptop to a network or another computer through an Ethernet cable. Your computer might also have a modem port, which you can plug a telephone line into, and then connect to the Internet, assuming you have an account with an Internet Service Provider (ISP). Both ports look very similar, so if you're unable to connect to your network or modem, verify that the cable is plugged into the right socket.	Chapters 7 and 8

Ports and jacks	Description and purpose	For more information, see
Microphone and headphone jacks Speaker, microphone and headphone jacks and a microphone jack	Your laptop is likely to have a headphone jack and a microphone jack. The headphone jack can also be used to connect your laptop to external speakers so that you enhance the sound of music.	Chapters 4 and 5
VGA port and cable Display adapter port Video cable	Your laptop should have a display adapter socket, which connects the video cable from an external monitor or projector to your laptop so that you can view your computer screen's image on another screen.	
Video output Composite video S-Video DVI	Your laptop might also have a video output port (such as an S-Video connector, composite video connector, or *DVI* connector) that can be used to connect to a television. Using an S-Video, composite video, or DVI connector and cable, you can display an image from your laptop directly onto a television set.	Chapter 7

Getting the Most Our of Your USB Ports

If you run out of USB ports on your laptop and want to connect more devices, you can either use a docking station (as described later in this chapter), or you can purchase a USB hub from a computer accessory retailer. A USB hub connects to one of your laptop USB ports, but provides additional ports (usually four to eight) to which you can connect more devices.

When you connect a USB device to a laptop for the first time, you usually have to install a program to enable the device. Refer to the documentation that comes with the device, and then follow the procedure necessary to connect it for the first time.

After the device has been set up, Windows XP recognizes it the next time you connect it.

Understanding Storage Devices

Most laptops come with two types of storage devices:

- *Hard disk drives.* They are the primary storage devices on your laptop. Hard disk drives come in a variety of sizes and are embedded inside the laptop.

  Important   Because the hard disk drive has spinning components, you should be careful about bumping, knocking, or dropping your laptop when it is turned on. Even though it's never advisable to kick or drop a mobile PC, the risk of damage is greatly minimized if the hard drive is not spinning.

- *External storage drives.*   You can also purchase a hard drive as a separate unit that connects to the computer with a USB or Ethernet cable. External hard disks are a cost effective way to expand the amount of storage for your mobile PC. They are also extremely useful as a place to back up all of the data from your mobile PC.

See Also   For more information on using the Windows XP Backup tool, see "Backing up Files and Folders" in Chapter 9, "Maintaining and Protecting Your Mobile PC."

- *Optical drives.*   If your laptop has an internal optical drive, you can most likely find it along one of the edges of the computer. You can read from and/or write to optical discs, such as CDs and DVDs. The type of optical drive your laptop might have varies.

  Tip   To find out what type of optical drive you have, look at the logo on the drive. For a complete list of available optical drives, refer to "More About Optical Drives" later in this chapter.

■   *External optical drives.*   Some models of mobile PCs ship with an optical drive as a separate unit that connects to the computer with a cable, or is built into the docking station. An external drive can be convenient because you can leave it behind to reduce the carrying weight of your mobile PC, but get all the functions of the optical drive when at your desk.

More About Optical Drives

Some newer drives offer the ability to record onto special types of disc. The proliferation of drive types has also led to the availability of different disc types. The table below presents the types of optical drives currently available and the discs they can read from and write to.

Type of optical drive	Type of discs
CD-ROM	CD-ROM, Music CD
DVD-ROM	CD-ROM, Music CD, DVD-ROM, DVD
CD-RW	CD-ROM, Music CD, CD-R
DVD+R, DVD+RW	CD-ROM, Music CD, CD-R, DVD-ROM, DVD, DVD+R, DVD+RW
DVD-R, DVD-RW and DVD-RAM	CD-ROM, Music CD, CD-R, DVD-ROM, DVD, DVD-R, DVD-RW, DVD-RAM

See Also   For more information about playing CDs and DVDs by using Microsoft Windows Media Player, see "Playing a Music CD on a Mobile PC" and "Watching a DVD on a Mobile PC" in Chapter 7, "At Home: Playing and Sharing Digital Media."

Understanding PC Cards

Most laptops have at least one socket that allows you to plug-in a *PC Card* (also called a *PCMCIA* card) to easily expand the capabilities of your computer. PC Cards are roughly the size of a credit card, and have a set of metal connectors on one end.

A wide variety of PC Cards are available from major computer accessory retailers, including the following:

■   *Wireless network card.*   Adds wireless networking capabilities to computers that don't have it built in.

■   *Global Positioning System (GPS) card.*   Enables your mobile PC to receive GPS information using compatible programs (such as Microsoft Streets and Trips 2005).

■ *Data/fax modem card.* Connects your mobile PC to the Internet by using a telephone line to send and receive faxes.

■ *Extra data storage card.* Expands the storage capabilities and size of your mobile PC.

■ *Video capture card.* Records video images from a camcorder or other video device.

■ *Fingerprint reader card.* Logs on to your computer by using your fingerprint rather than by typing in a user name and password.

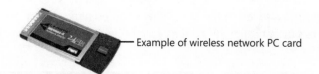
Example of wireless network PC card

Important If your laptop doesn't have built-in wireless capabilities, a PC Card can provide a quick and economic way to get wireless network access. For more information about wireless networks, see "Using Wireless Networking" in Chapter 3, "Introduction to Networking."

Understanding Docking Stations and Port Replicators

Because a laptop is limited in the amount of space that it has for ports and sockets, it usually relies on other devices to expand its capabilities. One very effective way to expand is to use a *dock* when using a laptop at your primary working location. For example, most mobile PCs come with one or two USB ports, and a typical dock comes with three or more.

Example of port replicator

There are two types of docks:

■ *Port replicators.* A port replicator is an attachment that extends the existing ports of your mobile PC so that you can connect external devices to it. A port replicator usually includes most of the following:

  ■ A VGA or DVI port (for an external monitor)

  ■ Ethernet (for network connection)

  ■ A serial port

- USB ports

- PS/2 ports (for keyboard and mouse)

- A parallel port (for printer connection)

- A headphone/speaker jack

- A microphone-in jack

- A power socket

- *Docking stations.* A docking station offers the same port extensibility that a port replicator does, but it also provides hardware components and expansion ports comparable to a desktop computer. In addition to the ports listed above, docking stations can include:

  - A CD/DVD-ROM drive

  - Extra disk storage

  - A wireless network card

  - PCMCIA ports (for adding other cards)

Important When you purchase a mobile PC, the manufacturer usually offers a docking station or a port replicator (but usually not both) as an optional extra. Refer to the documentation that comes with the docking station on how to connect it to your mobile PC.

For the rest of the book, we refer to any docking device as a docking station, but everything described and discussed is equally applicable to port replicators.

Using a Docking Station with Your Laptop

Docking stations come in a variety of designs. Some are a full cradle that the computer sits in, with a latch to lock the computer in place; others have a simple connection to hook into the computer. Some designs force you to close the lid on your laptop in order to dock; others can be used with the laptop lid open.

After you have connected all the appropriate cables to your docking station, you're ready to dock your mobile PC.

Tip A laptop can be docked whether it is on or off.

To locate the docking connector on your laptop, look at the back and bottom of your computer and identify the largest socket (usually 2 inches to 3 inches long), which is sometimes protected by a plastic flap.

Example of underside of a laptop

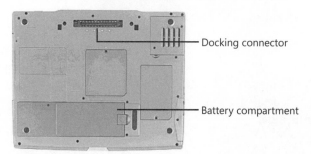

Docking connector

Battery compartment

To dock your laptop, look for the connector on the docking station that matches your mobile PC's connector, and then connect the two. When placing your laptop in the docking station, make sure that the connectors align properly and that any docking station latches are secured. A click signifies that the docking has been successful. If your computer was on when you docked it, Windows takes a few seconds to recognize the configuration (during which you might see the screen flicker a couple of times).

After you have docked your laptop, it has access to all of the connected external devices, effectively turning it into a desktop computer.

See Also For information on how to undock your computer, see "Undocking your Mobile PC" in Chapter 4, "Using Your Mobile PC At Your Desk."

Other Devices for Your Mobile PC

Although we have already covered some of the peripherals that can be connected to your mobile PC using the different ports and sockets, more devices are available. Below is a table of some of the most common devices and how they how they are usually connected.

Type of device	Description	Common port or socket	For more information, see:
Digital audio player	A device that stores and plays music copied from a computer.	USB	Chapter 7
Digital camera	A device that stores images digitally rather than on film. You can view, edit, and print the digital images.	USB	Chapter 7

Type of device	Description	Common port or socket	For more information, see:
USB flash drive	A small device that offers additional data storage and can be used to copy files onto and off of computers.	USB	Chapter 5
Webcam	A small camera that can be used to record video for transmission to someone else.	USB	
Personal digital assistant (PDA)	A handheld computer that provides a way to store and carry personal information. You can copy your e-mail messages, calendar, contact information, and documents to a PDA from a computer.	USB	Chapter 4
Mobile phone	A phone that you carry with you to make calls from different and even remote locations. You can copy your calendar and address book information stored on a computer to the mobile phone to save time.	USB or Bluetooth	Chapter 3 for more on Bluetooth

Working on a Tablet PC

Tablet PCs are great computers for mobile users. You can use a special pen to write in digital ink on the display screen, as well as navigate through Windows XP and interact with the user interface as you would with any other pointing devices. Using the pen, you can take handwritten notes in a meeting, create handwritten e-mails in Microsoft Office Outlook 2003, or send handwritten messages via MSN Messenger. You can also use the Tablet PC Input Panel to convert your handwritten content into text for use in any program.

Using a Tablet PC, you can:

- Take handwritten notes

- Convert your handwriting to text.

- Annotate documents in your handwriting.

■ View files in portrait or landscape orientation.

■ Execute tasks and actions using voice commands by taking advantage of the latest in speech recognition technology.

See Also For more information about using your Tablet PC, see "Entering Information by Using the Tablet PC Pen" in Chapter 4, "Using Your Mobile PC at Your Desk." For more information about using speech to interact with your Tablet PC, see "Recording Speech on Your Tablet PC" in Chapter 6, "Using Your Mobile PC at Home"

Selecting the Right Tablet PC for You

Just as you would review available models and types before buying a car so that it suits your needs and wants, you need to learn about the two main types of Tablet PCs before selecting the one that is right for you.

The following types of Tablet PCs are available:

■ *Slate.* Tablet PCs are ultra-slim and are used with an external keyboard or the pen. This type of Tablet PC offers maximum mobility because it is lightweight and easy to carry. You mainly interact with the slate using the pen, but the external keyboard can be carried with you. You can change the screen orientation to either portrait or landscape orientation. When you work at your desk, you can take full advantage of an external keyboard and mouse.

■ *Convertible.* A convertible Tablet PC has a built-in keyboard, much like a regular laptop, but its screen rotates and folds back so that it converts into a slate. You interact with the Tablet PC by using the pen when it's in slate mode, and by using the keyboard when it is in laptop mode. Convertible Tablet PCs offer the best of both worlds, but are usually a little larger and heavier.

Using a Tablet Pen

The Tablet pen can be used in the following situations:

■ As you would a mouse, to select menus and commands, to click buttons, and so forth.

■ To handwrite notes in ink-enabled programs, such as Microsoft OneNote 2003 or MSN Messenger.

■ To convert handwritten content to text for copying into any program.

See Also For more information about using the Tablet PC Input Panel to convert handwriting to text, see "Entering Information Using the Tablet PC Pen" in Chapter 4, "Using Your Mobile PC At Your Desk." For more information about sending ink messages by using MSN Messenger, see "Using Ink with MSN Messenger on Your Tablet PC" in Chapter 4, "Using Your Mobile PC At Your Desk." For more information about taking handwritten notes in meetings, see "Taking Notes on Your Tablet PC" in Chapter 5, "Using Your Mobile PC in Meetings."

In this exercise, you will learn how to use the Tablet pen to move the insertion point, as well as select and right-click items.

USE the *2005 Fall Catalog Ideas* document in the practice file folder for this topic. This practice file is located in the *My Documents\Microsoft Press\Laptops and Tablet PCs with Windows XP SBS \Hardware\UsingTabletPCPen* folder.

1 To display the current date in a ToolTip, using the Tablet pen, hover the pointer over the time in the notification area.

2 To hide the ToolTip, move the Tablet pen away from the notification area.

3 Double-tap the time in the notification area.

The Date and Time Properties dialog box appears.

4 In the **Date and Time Properties** dialog box, tap **OK**.

5 While hovering over the desktop, press and hold the button located on the side of your Tablet pen, and then tap **Properties**.

6 To close the **Display Properties** dialog box, click **Cancel**.

7 To open a program, tap **Start**, tap **All Programs**, tap **Accessories**, and then tap **WordPad**.

The WordPad window appears.

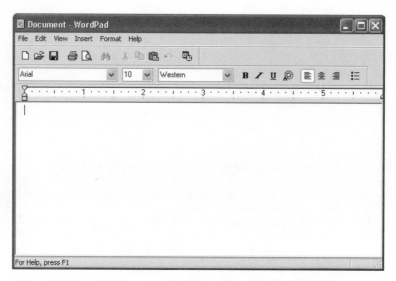

8 In the WordPad window, tap the **File** menu, and then tap **Open**.

9 In the **Open** dialog box, browse to the *My Documents\Microsoft Press\Laptops and Tablet PCs with Windows XP SBS\Hardware\UsingTabletPCPen* folder, and then double-tap **2005 Fall Catalog Ideas**.

10 Drag the pen to select the three lines of text.

11 To format the selected text as a bulleted list, press and hold the Tablet pen button while pointing to the selected text, and then tap **Bullet Style**.

Close

12 Tap the **Close** button.

13 When prompted to save the changes, tap **No**.

The following table summarizes the various pen actions that can be performed and the mouse equivalents.

Pen Action	Mouse Action
Hover over a target	Point
Tap	Click
Double-tap	Double-click
Press and hold Tablet pen button	Right-click

Changing Screen Orientation on a Tablet PC

Depending on what task you're performing and where you are using your Tablet PC, you might use it in either landscape or portrait orientation. For example, some documents are easier to read in Portrait mode, but wide documents, such as spreadsheets, are viewed better in Landscape mode.

Tablet PC in portrait orientation

Tablet PC in landscape orientation

You can change screen orientation by either using the hardware button or buttons located near the Tablet PC screen, or by using the "Change screen orientation" command.

In this exercise, you will adjust the screen orientation of your Tablet PC, as well as modify the application sequence in which the orientation changes.

BE SURE TO log on to your Tablet PC before beginning this exercise.

1   In the notification area, tap the **Change tablet and pen settings** icon.

2   To start rotating the screen orientation, tap **Change screen orientation**.

The screen orientation rotates 90 degrees.

3   To return your screen to its initial orientation, repeat steps 1 and 2 three times.

4   To configure the orientation sequence rather than use the default one, in the notification area, tap the **Change tablet and pen settings** icon, and then tap **Properties**.

5 In the **Tablet and Pen Settings** dialog box, tap the **Display** tab.

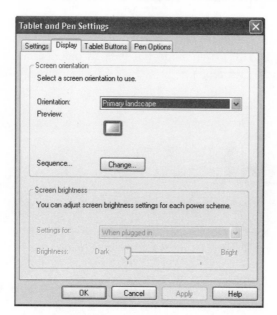

6 In the **Screen Orientation** area, tap the **Change** button.

7 In the **Orientation Sequence Settings** dialog box, tap the **2** arrow, and then tap **Secondary Landscape**.

8 Tap the **3** arrow, and then tap **Primary Portrait**.

9 To close the open dialog boxes and apply the new settings, double-tap **OK**.

10 To test the new sequence, in the notification area, tap the **Change tablet and pen settings** icon, and then tap **Change screen orientation**.

The screen orientation rotates 180 degrees.

11 To return to the original sequence, in the notification area, tap the **Change tablet and pen settings** icon, and then tap **Properties**.

12 In the **Screen Orientation** area in the **Tablet and Pen Settings** dialog box, click the **Change** button to the right of **Sequence**.

13 In the **Orientation Sequence Settings** dialog box, click the **2** arrow, and then click **Primary Portrait**.

14 Click the **3** down arrow, click **Secondary Landscape**, and then tap **OK**.

15 To close the **Tablet and Pen Settings** dialog box and apply the default settings, tap **OK**.

Effectively Managing Your Battery Power

When you are done using your mobile PC, you probably *shut down* your computer. But that means that the next time you want to use your mobile PC, you have to wait for a few seconds, or even minutes, for it to start up. If you move around a lot with your mobile PC, it can be frustrating to wait for the computer to start each time you want to use it. On the other hand, if you keep your mobile PC running, you know that you won't have enough battery power to last all day.

You can optimize both the battery life and start time or your mobile PC by taking advantage of three "off" modes that are available with Windows XP:

■ *Standby.* This mode turns off your computer, but keeps all of the information you were working on in memory so that you don't lose any work. Your mobile PC is configured to go to standby after the computer has been idle for a set period of time, or when you close the lid. You can also manually put your computer on standby. To "wake it up," you either press the power button on your computer or open the lid. It takes a few seconds for your computer to restore to the state it was in before going into standby mode.

■ *Hibernate.* This mode saves all your work to a special file on the hard disk and completely turns off the computer. All of your work is restored when you wake up the computer, which usually takes around 15 seconds. You can wake up your PC from Hibernate mode in the same way you wake it from Standby mode, by pressing the power button or opening the lid.

■ *Shutdown.* This mode completely shuts down the computer and doesn't save or store any of your work.

In this exercise, you'll enable your mobile PC to hibernate.

BE SURE TO log on to your Tablet PC before beginning this exercise.

1 Click **Start**, and then click **Control Panel**.

2 In Control Panel, click **Performance and Maintenance**.

3 In the Performance and Maintenance window, click **Power Options**.

> **Tip** Using the **Power Options** dialog box, you can also configure the settings that determine the length of inactivity before your computer goes into standby.

4 In the **Power Options** dialog box, click the **Hibernate** tab.

Important When traveling on an airplane, you are usually required to turn off your computer during take off and landing. You must therefore shutdown your computer rather than put it in Standby mode or Hibernate mode.

5 Select the **Enable Hibernate** check box and then click **OK**.

6 Click the **Close** button.

Close

Key Points

- It's important to be able to identify the key hardware components and the different ports and sockets of your laptop to fully take advantage of its capabilities, as well as troubleshoot any problems that come up.

- By configuring your computer to use ClearType, you can make text easier to read on your mobile PC screen.

- Tablet PCs are a new type of portable computer that you can interact with by using a special pen.

- The available types of Tablet PCs are a slate, which has no built-in keyboard, and a convertible, which has a built-in keyboard.

- Tablet PC screens can rotate and can be used in both Landscape and Portrait modes, depending on the type of work you are doing.

- Take advantage of the Standby and Hibernate modes to better manage power on your mobile PC and maximize your battery life.

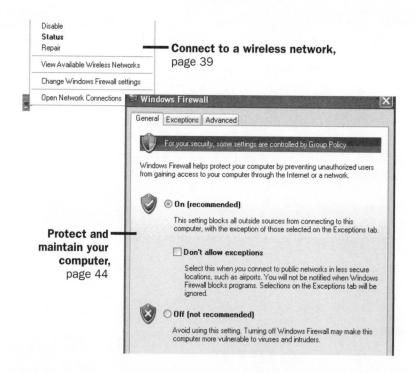

Connect to a wireless network,
page 39

Protect and maintain your computer,
page 44

Chapter 3 at a Glance

3 Introduction to Networking

In this chapter you will learn to:

✔ Understand basic networking.

✔ Connect to the Internet.

✔ Use broadband Internet.

✔ Compare broadband solutions.

✔ Use wireless networking.

✔ Connect to a wireless network.

✔ Use Bluetooth wireless technology.

✔ Compare 802.11 standards and Bluetooth.

✔ Protect and maintain your computer.

With the advent of e-mail and instant messaging, setting up a network is no longer a task just for techies. In the ever-changing world of technology, people need to collaborate, whether they are at home, at work, or traveling (on business or maybe even on vacation). Using a mobile PC, you can stay in touch with people, as well as remain productive, while on the go. Fortunately for computer users, Microsoft Windows XP was designed with networking in mind. You can use the built-in tools included in Windows XP to connect your mobile PC to small or large networks. The networked computers can have different operating systems, languages, and of course, locations, and still communicate and share resources over that network.

In this chapter, you will learn the fundamentals of networking and connecting to the Internet. You'll also learn about the different wireless technologies available for your mobile PC and how to protect your computer from potentially harmful content.

See Also   Do you need only a quick refresher on the topics in this chapter? See the Quick Reference entries on page xxi.

Understanding Basic Networking

Networking is the practice of linking computing devices together with hardware and software that supports data communications across the computing devices. Networks can be categorized in different ways. One of the most common ways to define the different types of networks is according to the geographic area it spans. *Local area networks* (LANs), for example, typically reach across a single location (such as an office or home), whereas *wide area networks* (WANs) reach across cities or states—or even across the world. The Internet is the world's largest public WAN.

Any computer that you want to network with other computers or add to an existing network must have a *network interface card* (NIC), also called a *network adaptor*. You can connect to a network either by physically plugging a cable into the NIC, or over a wireless connection. Most mobile PCs today enable either one or both types of connections.

Tip   If you want to create a home network, you will also need a *hub,* which is a device to which all the computers on the network connect.

In addition to the NIC, software-based network protocols must be set up on your computer. The most common suite of networking protocols is *Transmission Control Protocol/Internet Protocol* (TCP/IP). TCP/IP is used as the basic communication language to connect hosts and computers to the Internet.

Every computer on a TCP/IP network is assigned a unique identifier, called an *IP address,* composed of a set of four numbers in the format *X.X.X.X,* where *X* ranges from 0 to 255. IP addresses are logically divided into two parts: the network (the first or first and second numbers) and the system on the network. In addition to an IP address, every computer on a TCP/IP network is given a *subnet mask,* which is used to partition the network into segments and accurately route packets sent either to the local network or to a different network.

In this exercise, you will locate the IP address and subnet mask currently assigned to your computer.

BE SURE TO log on to Windows before beginning this exercise.

1   Click **Start**, and then click **Control Panel**.

2   In Control Panel, click the **Network and Internet Connections** link.

3   In the Network and Internet Connections window, click the **Network Connections** link.

4   In the Network Connections window, click your network connection icon.

   Tip   Typically, the icon is labeled either "Local Area Connection" or "Wireless Network Connection."

Your computer's IP address and subnet mask address are shown in the **Details** area on the left side of the window.

CLOSE the Network Connections window.

In addition to the IP address and subnet mask address, computers have a *domain name*. The main purpose of a domain name is to translate an alphabetic name into a numeric IP address and facilitate the entry of server names. For example, let's say the IP address of the server you want to reach is 131.107.255.254 and its domain name is *gardenco.msn.com*. Of course, it's much easier to remember the user-friendly domain name than the IP address.

Important   Like IP addresses, domain names must be unique, and require registration. Global databases store the mapping between the two. To register a domain name, visit an authorized registration site such as *www.networksolutions.org* or *www.register.com*.

In order to transfer information to the correct destination, a *gateway* must be able to identify and validate the IP address and subnet mask address of your computer against the address book stored on a *Domain Name System* (DNS) server. A DNS server maintains a central list of domain names (if applicable) and IP addresses, and maps the domain names in your Internet requests to other servers on the Internet.

Finally, in order to establish communication between networks, the networked computers need more than a protocol suite and addresses. They need a socket. A *socket* is a software object that connects a program to a network protocol or other computer on the Internet. You can have many sockets, including one each for *File Transfer Protocol (FTP)*, *Hypertext Transfer Protocol (HTTP)*, *Telnet*, and e-mail. After a connection is established through the socket, the client computer can use the services provided by the host.

Connecting to the Internet

Now that you have a basic understanding of networking, let's take a look at how you connect your computer to the Internet.

The most common way to connect to the Internet is with a modem and an Internet service provider (ISP) account. A *modem* is a hardware device that allows computers to communicate with each other by transmitting signals over telephone lines, enabling what is called "dial-up access." Modems come in different speeds—the higher the speed, the faster the data are transmitted.

For an overview of the different types of available modems, take a look at the following table.

Modem Type	Description
Analogs	A type of modem that connects a computer to the Internet through a phone line. Internal modems plug into a PCI port inside a computer. External modems plug into a serial port, parallel port, or USB port on a computer. A 56 kilobits per second (Kbps) modem can receive data at about 53 Kbps.
Integrated Services Digital Network (ISDN)	A type of modem that connects a computer to the Internet through a high-speed digital line installed by a telephone company or telecommunications provider.
Digital Subscriber Line (DSL)	A digital device that connects a computer or network to a larger network through telephone wiring using DSL techniques. Modem is actually a misnomer for this type of connection because there is no conversion from digital to analog.
Cable	A type of modem that connects to a local cable TV line to provide a continuous connection to the Internet. It can achieve transfer rates of about 1.5 megabits per second (Mbps). Cable modems attach to a 10Base-T Ethernet card port on your computer.

To connect your computer to the Internet, you must go through a service provider. You can connect to the service provider through:

- *A local area network (LAN).* A LAN is a computer network that spans only a small area. LANs are confined to a single building, groups of buildings, or range of a few miles.

- *A high speed broadband connection such as cable, ISDN or DSL.* Broadband Internet connections enable high-speed data transmission through a single cable. The most common types of broadband connections are cable modems and DSL modems. Because of its multiple-channel capacity, broadband has started to replace base-band, the single-channel technology originally used in most computer networks.

- *A dial-up connection.* A connection established between computers over a standard telephone line.

With the exception of cable or DSL connections, which typically do not require a user name and password, you need to use the New Connection Wizard to set up your connection. Before going through the wizard, make sure that you have the following information available from your service provider:

- Specific IP address or the address of the DHCP server
- DNS address and domain name

Important   To share your Internet connection with other computers on your network, consider using a high-speed modem such as DSL or cable. Ask your local telephone company or cable television provider whether these services are available in your area.

Using Broadband Internet

Because the Internet has become an integral part of people's lives and ongoing access to it is seen as a "necessity," most people are willing to pay their phone or cable company a monthly fee to get the fastest access possible.

Broadband is the term frequently used to describe faster Internet capability when compared with traditional modem dial-up Internet access. Broadband can be delivered through a range of technologies. These include:

- DSL
- Cable
- Radio/Microwave
- Satellite
- Wireless

Broadband tends to be more expensive than dial-up access or narrowband. Also, note that broadband access is not usually metered. This means you pay a monthly "flat" rate to access the Internet at any time without any call charges. With no per-call fees to pay, you know what your monthly bill is going to be. However, there may be installation costs that you would want to know about before signing up.

There are many advantages of high-speed Internet access, such as:

- The connection is always on, which means you can access the Internet without the need to dial your Internet service provider over a telephone line.
- Information can be downloaded into your computer at significantly higher speeds than traditional modems.
- You can go online without making your telephone line unavailable.

■ Employees can use broadband networks for video conferencing, and to make it easier to telecommute.

■ High bandwidth makes it less time-consuming to download or view entertainment.

Tip Broadband Internet connections are typically capable of transmitting at a speed of 512 Kbps or more.

How Does Broadband Work?

Broadband Internet access makes the data processing capabilities necessary to use the Internet available through one of several high-speed transmission technologies. These data processing capabilities are "digital" in nature, meaning that they compress vast amounts of voice, video, and data information, which are broken down into what are called "bits." These bits become words, pictures, etc., on your computer screen. The transmission technologies that make high-speed Internet access possible move these bits much more quickly than do traditional telephone or wireless connections.

Comparing Broadband Solutions

As you've probably figured out by now, a regular dial-up modem is a pretty slow way to connect to the Internet and broadband is more desirable. Unfortunately, it's neither as simple to get connected as it should be, nor as cheap as we would like. There are now a number of options and alternatives for getting connected, all of them offering different speeds and at different prices.

The following table presents information to help you choose the best broadband solution for your needs.

Broadband solution	Max download Speed	Max upload speed	Pros	Cons
xDSL	8 Mbps	1 Mbps	● Uses existing phone line ● Widely available	● May be expensive
Cable	30 Mbps	30 Mbps	● Doesn't need phone lines	● Shared bandwidth ● Limited availability

Broadband solution	Max download Speed	Max upload speed	Pros	Cons
ISDN	64 Kbps	64 Kbps	● Uses existing phone line ● Widely available	● Variable pricing models ● Limited speed
Radio/ Microwave	2 Mbps	2 Mbps	● Emerging technology	● Needs line of sight ● Limited speed ● Currently has limited coverage
Satellite	3 Mbps	56 Kbps	● Good speed ● Good coverage	● Needs phone line ● One way transmission – need a separate modem to upload. ● Not suitable for gaming

Using Wireless Networking

The increased use of laptop computers and Tablet PCs within corporations, small businesses, and even for personal use, and the increased mobility of people using these devices, has fueled the demand for wireless networks. Until recently, wireless technology was a patchwork of incompatible systems from a variety of vendors. The technology was slow and expensive. With the maturing of industry standards and the deployment of lightweight wireless networking hardware across a broad market section, wireless technology has come of age.

Wireless networking is a way to connect computers or other devices, either in your home or across long distances, using infrared light or radio frequency signals. There are two types of wireless networks:

- *Infrastructure network.*   A local area network that uses access points to connect computers and devices on the network.

- *Ad hoc network.*   A computer-to-computer local area network with several users in a limited area, such as a conference room.

Standards for wireless (802.11x) networks, also known as *Wireless Local Area Networks* (WLANs) or *wireless LANs*, are based on the original Ethernet design. WLANs operate in unlicensed frequency spectrums and thus are prey to performance lapses and security problems. For example:

- Anything with high water content would absorb 2.4-GHz radio frequency energy and decrease performance.

- A room containing stacks of papers can have transmission "shadows" or "dead spots," which would make connections unavailable in certain areas of the room.

- Microwave ovens, cordless phones, and satellite systems can affect performance by competing for frequency access.

Important   At the time of publishing this book, most WLANs are confined to small areas (about 500 feet), but various standardization committees are discussing additional wireless standards.

Even considering those drawbacks, WLANs are very useful in a variety of situations. For example, if you travel with a mobile computer, you can connect to the Internet through wireless access points installed in airports, hotels, coffee shops, libraries, and other public locations. You can also synchronize data and transfer files between two computers or between a computer and another device, such as a cell phone or a *personal digital assistant* (PDA).

Wireless Networking Pros and Cons

With a growing demand for easier and faster access to networks and the Internet, many people have added wireless capabilities also known as Wi-Fi to their broadband service. Although the potential for such 802.11-configured tools are almost limitless, people have begun to realize that the advantages unfortunately do come with some setbacks, as well.

The main advantages of wireless networking are:

- *Mobility.*   You can move about freely and still remain connected to your network and to the Internet.

- *Easy installation.*   The required network infrastructure, such as base stations and antennas, can be installed and configured almost anywhere, including places too difficult to set up wired networks.

- *Flexibility.*   Wireless networks easily scale to accommodate more users. Adding new users and/or computers to this type of network is also very simple and quick.

- *Troubleshooting.*   Problems can be more easily and quickly identified—they either exist at the end-user's station or at the base station (assuming that the high-speed Internet connection is readily available and working properly).

- *Cost savings.* When all the wireless network setup devices have been purchased, nothing else is required to maintain the network—no more wires, no more cables. Additions can be made easily without having to purchase any more material.

- *Standardization.* With its standardization and the greater variety of cards to choose from, wireless networks are competitively priced, causing prices to drop dramatically and making 802.11b a fairly cheap wireless networking solution for small or large networks.

The main disadvantages are:

- *Reliability.* The response time is usually much longer for wireless networks than it is for wired networks because data is continuously lost in cyberspace and requires retransmission.

- *Signal distortion.* Wireless signals received by computers are sometimes distorted or corrupted by environmental interference. This can also cause time delays. Sometimes, due to this interference, the path to a particular wireless device can be completely lost and no data transmission can take place. If, for example, a radio is using the same frequency as the network, the performance of the wireless network is degraded.

Connecting to a Wireless Network

Now that you have a basic understanding of wireless networking, let's take a look at what is required to establish a connection to a wireless network. You can establish connections to wireless networks from a variety of environments and locations, but the basic steps and process are always the same: you locate the network that you want to join, click the Connect button, and then provide any required information.

In this exercise, you will connect to a wireless network.

BE SURE TO be in range of at least one wireless network.

1   Click **Start**, and then click **Control Panel**.

2   In Control Panel, click the **Network and Internet Connections** link.

3   In the Network and Internet Connections window, click the **Network Connections** link.

4   In the Network Connections window, click your wireless network connection icon.

5 On the **Network Tasks** menu in the left pane of the **Network Connections** window, click **View available wireless networks**.

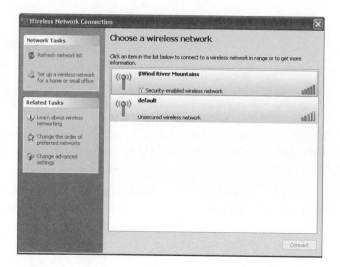

Important Some wireless networks might not appear on the list. If you know that you are in range of a specific wireless network and want to look for it, double-click the network connection icon in the notification area, and then in the Network Tasks area of the Wireless Network Connection dialog box, click **Refresh network list**.

6 In the **Choose a wireless network** list, click the wireless network to which you want to connect, and then click **Connect**.

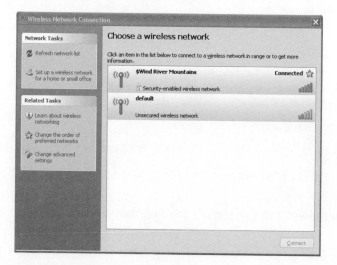

If the network you choose is security-enabled, the network key is either automatically provided by the network or system administrator (that is, the network supports IEEE 802.11x) and the connection is made automatically; or, you are prompted to manually type the network key.

Important   If the network is one that supports Wireless Provisioning Services, such as a public wireless network or a corporate network, you might be asked to download additional files that will allow your computer to connect to the network.

See Also   For more information about connecting to public hotspots, see "Connecting to a Public Network" in Chapter 8, "Traveling with Your Mobile PC."

CLOSE the Network Connections window.

Troubleshooting   Sometimes when you connect to a wireless network, you are prompted to enter the type of network connection, the name of the network, the encryption level, and the encryption key. The network is called the Service Set Identifies (SSID). The SSID is included with all transmissions to designate which network accepts the data. The network key, also called a wired equivalent privacy (WEP) key acts as a password that you use to gain access to the network. In some cases, the key might be provided to you by the network administrator. In other cases, you might be asked to create a key.

Troubleshooting   If you run into connectivity problems or lose your connection to your wireless network after it's been established, right click the wireless icon in the notification area, and then click **Repair** to have Windows try to reestablish the connection to the network.

Using Bluetooth Wireless Technology

Bluetooth wireless technology was designed primarily to support simple wireless networking of personal consumer devices and peripherals, such as cell phones, PDAs, printers, keyboards, mice, and wireless headsets. Bluetooth operates over a short distance (typically up to 30 feet) and uses radio transmission to enable wireless communication between devices.

Bluetooth wireless technology is used to:

- Create wireless connections to the Internet with a mobile phone or a modem server.

- Transfer files between computers or between a computer and another device.

- Print to a Bluetooth wireless printer.

- Enable a Bluetooth wireless keyboard and mouse.

- Join a personal area network (PAN).

- Synchronize PDAs to a computer or other device.

The data transfer speed for Bluetooth wireless technology can be up to 700 Kbps per second, but varies depending on the device or environmental factors. A Bluetooth device can transmit through walls, pockets, and briefcases.

Important   Although the Bluetooth standard uses the same 2.4 GHz range as 802.11b and 802.11g, Bluetooth technology is not a suitable Wi-Fi replacement. Compared to Wi-Fi, Bluetooth networking is much slower, a bit more limited in range, and supports fewer devices.

To install your Bluetooth device, refer to the instructions that came with the device. To determine whether you have Bluetooth built into your mobile computer, open Control Panel and look for a Bluetooth Devices icon. The Bluetooth radio transmitter installed on your computer appears as a network connection in the Network Connections window, just like any other type of network connection.

Comparing 802.11 Standards and Bluetooth

When evaluating your options and deciding on the best wireless technology to adopt, you face some difficult choices. A wide variety of products that conform to different wireless standards, such as 802.11a, 802.11b, 802.11g, and Bluetooth, are readily available. To make an educated network building decision, it's important to understand the relative pros and cons of each of these technologies.

Technology	Definition	Pros	Cons
802.11	The first WLAN standard created by the Institute of Electrical and Electronics Engineers (IEEE) in 1997.		● Supported a maximum bandwidth of 2 Mbps–too slow for most programs ● No longer being manufactured
802.11a	Second extension of the 802.11 standard developed by IEEE. Supports bandwidth up to 54 Mbps and signals in a regulated 5 GHz range.	● Fast maximum speed ● Supports a large number of simultaneous users ● Regulated frequencies prevent signal interference from other devices	● High cost ● Shorter range signal is easily obstructed
802.11b	First extension of the 802.11 standard. Created by IEEE in 1999. Supports bandwidth up to 11 Mbps, comparable to traditional Ethernet.	● Lowest cost ● Good signal range ● Not easily obstructed	● Slow maximum speed ● Supports a limited number of simultaneous users ● Appliances may interfere on the unregulated frequency band

Technology	Definition	Pros	Cons
802.11g	Combines the best of both 802.11a and 802.11b by supporting bandwidth up to 54 Mbps, and using the 2.4 GHz frequency for greater range. Backward-compatible with 802.11b and works with 802.11b wireless network adapters.	● Fast maximum speed ● Supports a large number of simultaneous users ● Good signal range ● Not easily obstructed	● Costs more than 802.11b ● Appliances may interfere on the unregulated signal frequency
Bluetooth	Alternative wireless network technology that supports a very short range (approximately 10 meters) and relatively low bandwidth (1 Mbps).	● Well suited for PDAs and cell phones	● Not well suited for mobile PCs ● Low bandwidth

Protecting and Maintaining Your Computer

Before you connect to the Internet, it is important to prepare your computer by installing the following:

■ *An Internet firewall.* A software or hardware security system that deters hackers, viruses, and worms from reaching your computer over the Internet.

■ *Antivirus software.* A program designed to detect and remove computer viruses. The simplest kind scans executable files and boot blocks for a list of known viruses. Others are constantly active, attempting to detect the actions of general classes of viruses. Antivirus software should always include a regular update service allowing it to stay current with the latest viruses.

Important After your computer is ready to face the Internet world, you still need to regularly maintain it to ensure that you have the latest available updates for both your antivirus software and your operating system.

See Also For additional tips on protecting your computer, see "Protecting Your Computer Against Spyware" in Chapter 9, "Maintaining and Protecting Your Mobile PC."

Using a Firewall

A firewall is a set of programs that filters all network packets to determine whether to forward them toward their destination. Firewalls are often installed away from the rest of the network so that no incoming request can get directly at private network resources. For mobile users, firewalls allow remote access to the private network through the use of secure logon procedures and authentication certificates.

There are two types of firewalls:

- *Hardware firewalls.* Many wireless access points and broadband routers for home networking have built-in hardware firewalls, which provide good protection for most home networks. The Microsoft Broadband Networking Wireless Base Station is one example of a wireless access point with a built-in hardware firewall and other integrated home networking features.

- *Software firewalls.* Firewalls are designed to "hide" your computer when it goes online, thus helping to protect your computer (and your privacy). A firewall can also detect traffic and analyze where it is going or coming from. If the location is suspect, then that traffic can be blocked. When a location is blocked, your firewall can create a log file that records the addresses and names of sites attempting to invade your computer. If necessary, a firewall can also dynamically open ports and allow your computer to receive traffic that you have specifically requested, such as a Web page address that you have clicked.

The Windows Firewall can block useful tasks, such as sharing files or printers through a network, transferring files in applications (for example, instant messaging), or hosting multiplayer games. Nonetheless, Microsoft recommends that you use a firewall to help protect your computer.

In this exercise, you will turn on the built-in firewall for an existing connection.

Important If you're using Windows XP SP2 or later, Windows Firewall might already be turned on.

1   Click **Start**, and then click **Control Panel**.

2   In Control Panel click the **Security Center** link.

3   In the Windows Security Center window click **Windows Firewall**.

4   In the **Windows Firewall** dialog box, select the **On (recommended)** option.

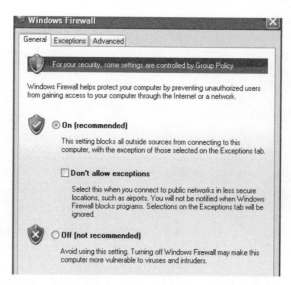

5   To apply the new settings, click **OK**.

Important   Windows Firewall will help protect a computer on a wireless network, but will not restrict access to the network itself. You should configure your wireless network to use a network key using either Wi-Fi Protected Access (WPA) or WEP.

Using Up-to-Date Antivirus Software

You may unwittingly bring a virus onto your computer through the Internet or through e-mail attachments. Antivirus software helps protect your computer against viruses. Many computers come with antivirus software installed, but you can also purchase antivirus software and install it yourself. If you notice unusual messages on your screen, decreased system performance, missing data, or inability to access your hard drive, run your virus-detection software immediately to minimize the chances of losing data. Programs on floppy disks may also contain viruses. Scan all floppy disks before copying or opening files from them, or starting your computer from them. Just having an antivirus program installed is not enough, however. You also need to keep your antivirus software up to date as new viruses are created every day.

In this exercise, you will search for antivirus software installed on your computer, and then verify that it is up-to-date.

BE SURE TO install antivirus software before beginning this exercise.

1 Click **Start**, point to **All Programs**, and then look for the word "virus" in the program list.

Tip You might also see the name of a popular antivirus manufacturer or package. These include McAfee, Norton, Trend Micro, and Symantec.

2 To verify that your antivirus software is up-to-date, click the program name on the **All Programs** menu.

3 In the anti-virus program window, click the **Help** menu, and then click the **Version Information** command (or equivalent).

4 Look for the update status and the date of the last update.

If you still aren't sure whether your antivirus software is up to date, go to your anti-virus software provider's Web site and cross-check the date of the latest available updates with the date of your last downloaded update.

Important Having two different antivirus programs installed on one computer can cause conflicts on your computer. Always uninstall existing antivirus software before installing another.

Key Points

- While traveling, you can connect your mobile computer to the Internet through wireless access points installed in airports, hotels, coffee shops, libraries, and other public locations.

- You need to carefully weigh your needs for connectivity with the available options and associated costs before selecting the best solution for you.

- Wireless networking provides you with almost continuous Internet connectivity at home, at work or when you are on the road, as well as increased mobility and flexibility, and reduced installation and support costs. Also, by installing and using Windows Firewall built into Windows XP SP2, you can reduce the security risks sometimes associated with wireless networking.

- Protecting and maintaining your mobile PC on a regular basis will ensure the safety of your computer as well as the security of your files and programs. Firewalls and antivirus software are two tools that you can use to achieve this goal.

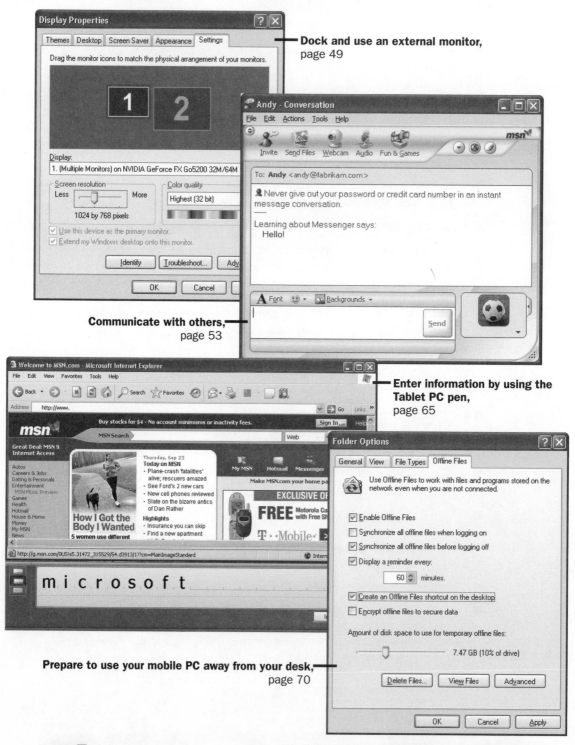

Dock and use an external monitor, page 49

Communicate with others, page 53

Enter information by using the Tablet PC pen, page 65

Prepare to use your mobile PC away from your desk, page 70

Chapter 4 at a Glance

4 Using Your Mobile PC at Your Desk

In this chapter you will learn to:

✔ Dock and use an external monitor.

✔ Communicate with others.

✔ Enter information by using the Tablet PC pen.

✔ Prepare to use your mobile PC away from your desk.

Whether you use your mobile PC in an office or at home, it is likely that you have a location (usually a stationary desk) where you use it the most.

In this chapter, you will learn how to take advantage of an external monitor at your desk to make working with your mobile PC for prolonged periods easier, how to set up your mobile PC so that you can work efficiently while away from your desk, and how to ensure that you have the files you need with you when you're ready to leave your office. You will also learn how to send quick messages to colleagues or friends and share files by using MSN Messenger.

For Tablet PC users, this chapter introduces the ink input enhancements available in Microsoft Windows XP Tablet PC Edition 2005.

See Also   Do you need only a quick refresher on the topics in this chapter? See the Quick Reference entries on pages xxi–xxv.

Important   Before you can use the practice files in this chapter, you need to install them from the book's companion CD to their default location. See "Using the Book's CD-ROM," on page xiii for more information.

Docking and Using an External Monitor

Although mobile PCs make great productivity tools and excellent entertainment devices, they do have some shortcomings that sometimes make them less than ideal for extended use. Most mobile PC screens are a little too small to comfortably read from and many don't have a full-size keyboard or a mouse. You generally have the option to plug a monitor, a keyboard, or a mouse directly into your mobile PC, but then when you want to leave your desk, you have to disconnect everything.

A convenient way to connect external devices, such as a monitor, a keyboard, or a printer, to your mobile PC is to use a docking station. Docking stations save you the hassle of connecting and disconnecting cables every time you take your PC away from your desk. The cables from the external devices connect to ports on the docking station, making it possible for you to have quick access to these devices when you dock your mobile PC.

See Also For more information on docking stations, see "Understanding Docking Stations and Port Replicators" in Chapter 2, "Getting to Know Your Mobile PC Hardware."

Docking stations include VGA ports to connect to an external monitor. The conventional way to use this monitor is to close the lid on your mobile PC and use just the external monitor.

Tip Although this section refers to using a docking station to connect your computer to an external monitor, you can plug the monitor directly into the VGA port of the laptop if you don't have a docking station available.

You also have the option of using both your mobile PC screen and an external monitor simultaneously. Windows XP allows you to configure settings to use both. Using two screens gives you additional flexibility and more screen space to arrange and view your programs and windows. If there is one program that you use more than others, display it on the larger monitor for easier viewing.

Tip You might find it useful to have your e-mail program and instant messaging service always open on one monitor so that you can easily keep track of incoming e-mail messages or quickly verify the availability of your co-workers or friends, while using your other screen to continue working in another program.

Tip Most of the Tablet PC docking stations are designed for viewing the computer in slate mode while it is docked. In this configuration, you can still take notes or make annotations on your Tablet PC screen and use other programs on the external monitor.

In this exercise, you will configure your mobile PC to use an external monitor in extended desktop mode.

Tip This exercise shows you how you can increase your productivity at your desk by using extended desktop mode. A similar exercise in Chapter 5 shows you how to use extended desktop mode to give a more polished presentation.

BE SURE TO position your mobile PC and desktop monitor relatively close together to ensure swifter navigation between screens. It doesn't matter on which side of the monitor you place the mobile PC because you can manually configure these settings.

1 Right-click the desktop, click **Properties**, and then click the **Settings** tab.

Two blue rectangles represent your displays and Monitor 2 (your external monitor) is unavailable because it hasn't yet been enabled.

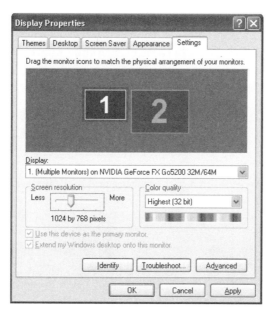

2 To enable Monitor 2, click its visual representation, and then select the **Extend my Windows desktop onto this monitor** check box.

Tip By default, Windows assumes that Monitor 2 is to the right of Monitor 1 (your mobile PC screen). If this isn't the case, drag the image of Monitor 1 or Monitor 2 into the appropriate position.

3 In the **Screen resolution** area, drag the slider to the right to change the screen resolution for Monitor 2 to **1024 by 768 pixels**, and then click **OK**.

4 When prompted to confirm that you want to keep the new settings, click **Yes**.

Troubleshooting If the external monitor is not showing your desktop background, click **No**, and then repeat step 3, but with a lower screen resolution.

More About the Primary Monitor

You might have noticed the "Use this device as the primary monitor" check box on the Settings tab of the Display Properties dialog box and wondering what a primary monitor is. In short, it is the first monitor that Windows uses when it starts up your computer. It's the monitor on which the logon screen and taskbar appear; programs open for the first time; and most dialog boxes and notifications are shown. On a mobile PC, the primary monitor is set by default to Monitor 1, which is always the mobile PC screen.

It is not recommended to change the default setting (and some mobile PCs prevent you from doing it) because it can cause problems when you undock.

When you first enable extended desktop mode, your mobile PC screen continues to show your desktop with the taskbar and any desktop icons you might have, while the external monitor only shows your desktop background. You might find it easier to use extended desktop mode when you have the taskbar on the external monitor, rather than on the smaller mobile PC screen.

In this exercise you will move the taskbar to the external monitor.

BE SURE TO have an external monitor available to which you can connect your mobile PC, before beginning this exercise.

1 Right-click on an empty area of the taskbar, and then click **Lock the Taskbar** to clear the selection.

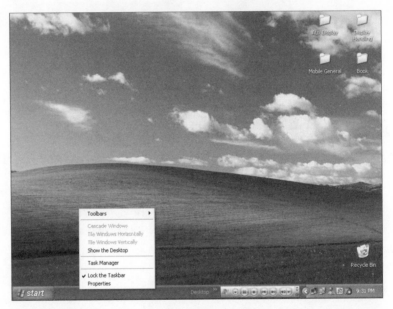

2 Drag the taskbar to the external monitor.

The taskbar now appears at the bottom of the external monitor screen.

Tip When you undock your computer, the taskbar moves back to your mobile PC screen. You will need to move it back to the external monitor when you dock again.

Now that you have the external monitor working as an extension of the desktop on your mobile PC screen, you can take advantage of the extra screen to drag programs onto the external monitor. You can also resize windows to stretch across multiple displays, which can be particularly useful for programs that contain large amounts of data (such as a large Microsoft Excel worksheet).

Tip A window cannot be dragged if it is maximized. If you are unable to move a program window to another monitor, click the **Restore** button, and then try to drag it again.

Restore

Communicating with Others

One of the great advantages of mobile PCs is that you can use them to keep in touch and share information with friends or colleagues at all times—even when you're away from your desk. You are no doubt familiar with using e-mail messaging as a way to communicate with other people, but another way to take advantage of your computer is to use instant messaging programs to send files, text messages, and video to other people as well as share programs.

Microsoft offers two main instant messaging programs: Microsoft Windows Messenger, which is included with Windows XP, and MSN Messenger, which you can download from the MSN Web site. Using MSN Messenger on a Tablet PC, you can even send handwritten messages.

Installing MSN Messenger

In this exercise, you will create a .NET Passport account and link it to your Windows XP user account, and then install the latest version of MSN Messenger.

BE SURE TO have an active Internet connection before beginning this exercise.

Tip This exercise assumes that you don't yet have an e-mail account; if you do skip to step 14.

1 Click **Start**, and then click **Control Panel**.

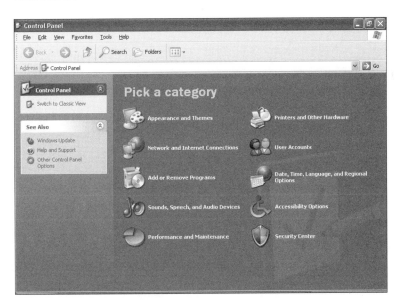

2 In Control Panel, click the **User Accounts** link.

3 In the User Accounts window, click the **User Accounts** link.

4 In the **User Accounts** dialog box click the **Advanced** tab, and then click **.NET Passport Wizard**.

5 On the first page of the .NET Passport Wizard, click **Next**.

6 On the **Do you have an e-mail address** page, click **No, I would like to open an MSN Hotmail account** and click **Next**.

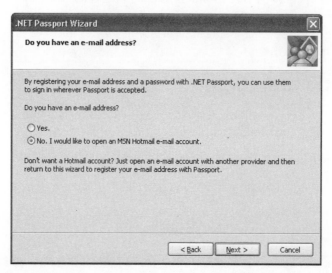

7 On the **Register with Hotmail and .NET Passport** page, click **Next**.

8 In the Get a .NET Passport window, fill in the registration information, read through the Hotmail Agreements section, and then click **I Agree**.

Tip When creating a password, it is good security practice to ensure that it contains a mix of both upper and lower case letters, numbers, and symbols.

9 On the **Registration is Complete** page, click **Continue**.

10 On the **Associate Your .NET Passport** page, click **Next**.

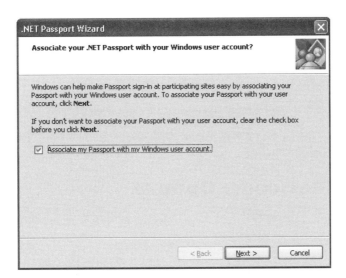

Important   By default, Windows associates this e-mail address with your Windows XP user account. This association enables Windows Messenger to connect when you log on to Windows, eliminating the need for you to re-enter your e-mail address and password.

11   On the **You're done!** page, click **Finish**.

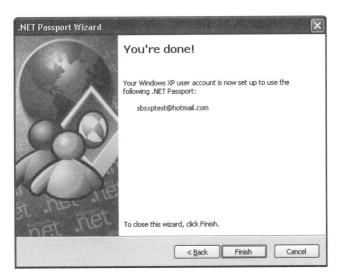

12   In the **User Accounts** dialog box, click **OK**.

13   Click the **Close** button.

Close

14 To install the latest version of MSN Messenger, click **Start**, and then click **Internet Explorer**.

15 In the Address Bar of the Internet Explorer window, type http://messenger.msn.com.

16 On the **MSN Messenger** page, click **Download Now**.

17 In the **Registered MSN User** area of the **Download MSN Messenger** page, click **Go**.

18 On the **Get started with MSN Messenger** page, follow the instructions to complete the download.

Setting MSN Messenger Options

Now that you've installed MSN Messenger, you're ready to start using it to communicate with people. Using MSN Messenger, you can:

- Let your contacts see your online status. The available options are:

  - Online: Ready to receive messages and converse.

  - Busy: At your computer, but not available for conversation.

  - Be Right Back: Away from your computer for a short period of time.

  - Away: Away from your computer and unavailable for conversation.

  Tip You can manually set your status to Away when you step away from your computer, or your status will automatically change to Away when you've been inactive for a set period of time.

  - On The Phone: At your computer, but conversing on the phone.

  - Out To Lunch: Away from your computer for about an hour.

  - Offline: Away from your computer for an extended period of time (such as when you leave your office at the end of the work day and won't be using your computer until the next morning).

- Type a message and send it to one or more of your contacts (assuming they are online).

- Personalize messages you send by changing the font and text color, as well as add emoticons—small icons that convey emotions and spice up messages.

- Send files to and receive files from contacts.

- Send a video image of yourself using a Web cam as well as receive video images from others (if they have a Web cam).

- Share a program with a contact so that both of you can interact with it.

■ Access other services, such as games and alerts.

■ Handwrite messages to your contacts, if you're using a Tablet PC.

In this exercise, you will sign into MSN Messenger, customize your name, select a personalized picture, and then add a contact.

BE SURE TO have the e-mail address of a contact who is also using MSN Messenger.

1 Click **Start**, point to **All Programs**, and then click **MSN Messenger**.

The MSN Messenger window appears.

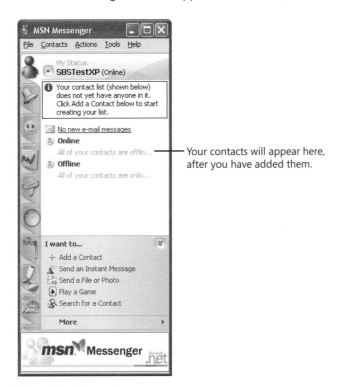

Your contacts will appear here, after you have added them.

Troubleshooting If MSN Messenger doesn't automatically sign you in, click the Sign In button, and then in the **.NET Messenger Service** dialog box, enter your e-mail address and password.

2 In the MSN Messenger window, click the **Tools** menu, and then click **Options**.

The Options dialog box appears.

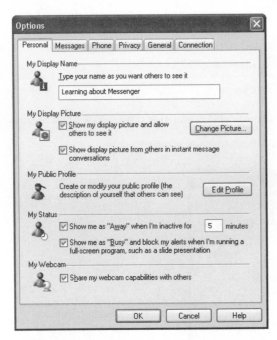

3 In the **Type your name as you want others to see it** box, type Learning about Messenger.

Tip Feel free to be creative when choosing a display name. Some people change their display name almost daily to reflect their mood of the day or to reflect what's going on in their lives.

4 In the **My Display Picture** area, click **Change Picture**.

5 In the **My Personal Picture** dialog box, in the list of images, click **Orange Daisy**, and then click **OK**.

The image appears to the right of your messages when you start a conversation with your contacts.

Tip You're not limited to the pictures that come with Windows XP. You can use a personal picture as your display picture by clicking **Browse** in the **My Personal Picture** dialog box, locating the desired picture, and then clicking **OK**.

6 In the **Options** dialog box, click **OK**.

7 In the MSN Messenger window, click the **Add a Contact** link at the bottom of the window.

The Add a Contact Wizard appears.

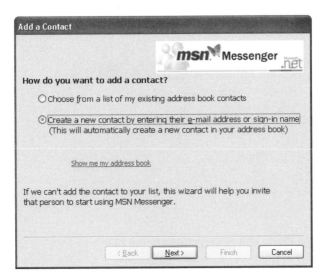

8 In the **Add a Contact** dialog box, select the **Create a new contact by entering their e-mail address or sign-in name** option, and then click **Next**.

9 In the **Please type your contact's complete e-mail address** box, type the e-mail address of the contact you wish to add or type someone@microsoft.com, and then click **Next**.

10 On the last page of the wizard, click **Finish**.

Note From the last page of the wizard, you can also choose to send an e-mail message to the newly added contact to let them know that you have added them to your contact list. The e-mail message includes a link to the MSN Messenger Web site from which they can download the latest version of MSN Messenger, if they haven't already done so.

Close

● On the MSN Messenger title bar, click the **Close** button.

MSN Messenger appears as a small icon in the notification area. A note displays above the icon when you receive a message.

The MSN Messenger icon will appear here when it is minimized.

When people add you to their contact list, a dialog box similar to the one shown below appears.

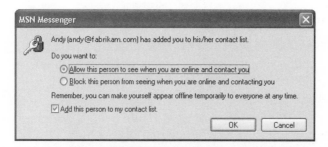

You can then choose to either add the person to your contact list or block them.

Tip You can delete any contact from your contact list by right-clicking the contact's name in the list and then clicking **Delete Contact**.

Sending Messages and Files by Using MSN Messenger

MSN Messenger provides an easy way to send messages to a friend or colleague. Messages you type are sent instantly, and replies are shown on your computer, allowing you to have an ongoing conversation. You can also choose to send them a files and links in the instant messaging window.

In this exercise, you will start a conversation with an online contact, send a file, and share an electronic whiteboard.

BE SURE TO have at least one online contact in your MSN Messenger contacts list, and ask that contact if he or she would mind assisting you before beginning this exercise.
USE the *Cat* picture in the practice file folder for this topic. This practice file is located in the *My Documents\Microsoft Press\Laptops and Tablet PCs with Windows XP SBS\Working\SendingFiles* folder.

1 Double-click on the **MSN Messenger** icon in the notification area.

The MSN Messenger window appears.

2   In the MSN Messenger window, double-click the name of an online contact with whom you want to start a conversation.

3   In the Conversation window, type **Hello!**, and then click **Send**.

The typed message appears in the conversation window.

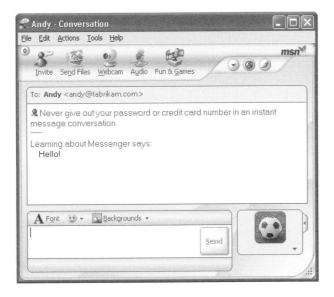

4   Wait for your contact's answer to appear in the conversation window, preceded by his or her name, and then type Thanks for helping me with this exercise.

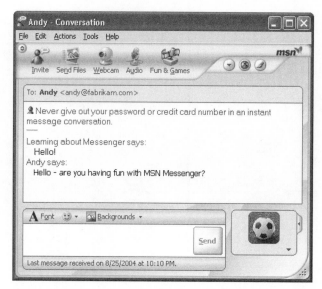

5   Click the **Select an emoticon** button above the text input area, click the **Smiley :)** icon in the upper-left corner of the dialog box, and then click **Send**.

Tip   Emoticons are a great way to make sure that the recipient of the message understands any jokes or other comments you make. If you want to make sure that your contact knows you are making a joke, use a smiley icon.

6   To send a file to a contact, in the **I want to** area at the bottom of the MSN Messenger window, click the **Send a File or Photo** link.

The Send a File or Photo dialog box appears.

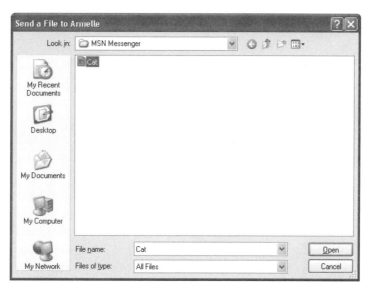

7 In the **Send a File** dialog box, click the name of the contact with whom you want to share the file, and then click **OK**.

8 In the **Send a File** dialog box, browse to the *My Documents\Microsoft Press \Windows XP for Laptops and Tablets\Working\SendingFiles* folder, click **Cat**, and then click **Open**.

MSN Messenger sends a message to the contact asking him or her to accept the file. When he or she accepts, a progress bar appears that indicates the transfer progress of the file.

9 To share a whiteboard with your contact, click the **Action** menu, and then click **Start Whiteboard**.

An invitation is sent to your contact. When it has been accepted, the Sharing Session box appears on your screen and the Whiteboard program opens. Anything you draw or type in the Whiteboard program is shared with your contact, and vice versa.

Important If you're using Windows XP SP2 with default settings, the first time you try running the Whiteboard program, the Windows Firewall attempts to block it from opening. When prompted, click the **Unblock** button to continue.

10 Type **What a great tool this is for collaborative work!**

Tip You can preserve the contents of the Whiteboard by clicking the **View** menu, and then clicking **Lock Contents**.

CLOSE Whiteboard and the Conversation window to end the conversation.

Using Ink with MSN Messenger on Your Tablet PC

MSN Messenger supports a great new feature on Tablet PCs. Rather than typing a message to a contact, you can send a handwritten message. To try this, follow these steps:

1 Double-click the **MSN Messenger** icon in the notification area.

2 In the MSN Messenger window, double-click the name of an online contact with whom you wish to start a conversation.

Click the Handwrite tab to send a message.

3   In the Conversation window, click the **Handwrite** tab.

4   Using the Tablet pen, handwrite Hello, and then click **Send**.

The message that you handwrote appears in the conversation window.

Important   Handwritten messages can be sent only to contacts running MSN Messenger version 6.0 or later. Handwritten content sent to contacts running older versions converts to typed text.

CLOSE all windows to end the conversation.

Entering Information by Using the Tablet PC Pen

If you have a Tablet PC, you are probably familiar with inputting text and writing notes by using the Tablet pen. By upgrading to Windows XP Tablet PC Edition 2005, you can take advantage of new capabilities that make it easier to use the Tablet pen to enter information.

These capabilities include the following:

■   You can access and use the Tablet PC Input Panel from anywhere on the screen (rather than docked at the bottom of the screen).

■   Input Panel immediately converts your handwriting to text and offers spelling suggestions for unrecognized words.

■ Using Input Panel, you can edit converted ink content before inserting it into an active program.

■ Input Panel can predict the type of data you are entering, based on the program you're currently using. For example, when your cursor is placed in the Address Bar of Internet Explorer, Input Panel provides useful options for entering a Web site address.

See Also   For more information about updating your mobile PC to Windows XP Service Pack 2, see "Upgrading to Windows XP Service Pack 2" in Chapter 1, "Running Microsoft Windows XP on a Mobile PC." To learn more about taking notes using the Tablet pen, see "Taking Notes on Your Tablet PC" in Chapter 5, "Using Your Mobile PC in Meetings."

In this exercise, you will use the new Tablet PC Input Panel to enter and correct text in Notepad, as well as enter a Web site address in a Web browser.

BE SURE TO install Windows XP Tablet PC Edition 2005 on your Tablet PC before beginning this exercise.

1   Tap **Start**, tap **All Programs**, tap **Accessories**, and then tap **Notepad**.

2   Tap where you want to insert text and keep the tip of the tablet pen close to the screen.

The **Tablet PC Input Panel** icon appears to the right of the insertion point.

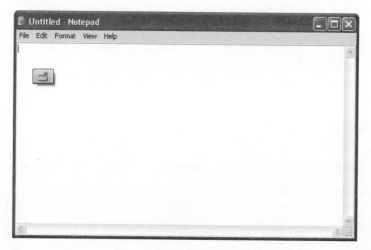

3   To open Input Panel, tap the **Tablet PC Input Panel** icon.

Writing pad

Writing Pad

4   In Input Panel, tap the **Writing Pad** button.

5   On the character pad, write It is easy to enter text using the new Tablet PC Input Panel.

As you write, each word converts to typed text and appears below the handwritten content.

Troubleshooting   If a word is not correctly recognized, click on the typed word, review the list of suggestions, and then either tap the correct word, or make the necessary adjustments in the correction area. When you have made a selection, tap **OK**.

6   To insert the text into the active Notepad document, tap **Insert**.

7   In Input Panel, tap the **On-Screen Keyboard** button.

On-Screen
Keyboard

8   Using the on-screen keyboard, type And I am entering text using the on-screen keyboard.

The text immediately appears in the Notepad.

Tip   You can use the arrow keys on the on-screen keyboard to move the insertion point if you need to make corrections.

Close

9   Tap the **Close** button.

10   Tap **Start**, and then tap **Internet Explorer**.

11   In the Internet Explorer window, tap the **Address Bar**.

A small icon appears to the right of the Address Bar.

Character Pad

12 Tap the **Tablet PC Input Panel** icon, and then tap the **Character Pad** button.

Writing pad   Web address buttons

13 To expedite the entry of the Web site address, tap **http://**, and then tap **www.**

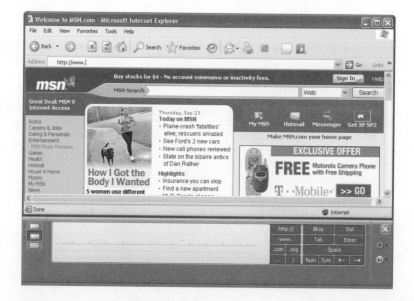

14 By tapping the characters in the character pad, write microsoft.

As you enter each character, Input Panel converts it to typed text.

Troubleshooting   If Input Panel hasn't recognized a character, tap the arrow that appears below the character and then tap the correct character in the list of alternates. If the character you want doesn't appear, tap **Clear** at the bottom of the list, and then rewrite the character.

15 After Input Panel recognizes the word *microsoft* and inserts it in the Address Bar, tap .com, and then tap **Insert**.

16   To open the Web page, tap **Go**.

CLOSE Internet Explorer.

Preparing to Use Your Mobile PC Away from Your Desk

While you are at your desk, your mobile PC is often connected to a power supply and the Internet. You can work without concerns about finding a power source or accessing files and information that you need. However, when you take your mobile PC away from your desk, you might be offline for a period of time, and therefore not have access to the files you need. You might also be away for longer than the charge-life of your battery and can't be sure that you'll have access to a power outlet, so it's always prudent to bring your power adapter along.

If you have a personal digital assistant (PDA) or mobile phone, you might want to ensure that it has the latest information from your mobile PC before you go offline so that you can use it as a reference when your mobile PC is either turned off or on standby.

Synchronizing Information with a PDA or Mobile Phone

If you carry a PDA, such as a Microsoft Windows Mobile Pocket PC, or a modern mobile phone, you can synchronize information from your mobile PC so that you can access it when you are away from your desk. The most commonly synchronized types of information are:

■ *Contacts details.*   The names, telephone numbers, and addresses of your contacts. This is particularly useful on a mobile phone because you can dial contacts without having to remember their telephone number. Synchronizing with the computer means that you only need to enter the details once.

■ *Calendar appointments.*   The time, date, and location of the appointments on your calendar. When synchronized with the latest information, your PDA or mobile phone gives you a reminder before your next appointment.

■ *E-mail.*   You can often synchronize your latest e-mails (usually without attachments) so that you can read them on your PDA or mobile phone. Note that e-mail can be awkward to read on a mobile phone due to the size of the screen.

■ *Music.*   Most PDAs and some mobile phones can play back digital audio files such as Microsoft Windows Media Audio (*WMA*) and *MP3* files. These files can be copied from your computer and then played using your PDA or mobile phone.

There are several ways to connect your mobile PC to a PDA or mobile phone. The most common way is to use a cradle or cable that usually comes with the PDA or mobile phone and connects to one of the USB ports on the mobile PC. You can also establish a connection with the PDA or mobile phone by using Bluetooth. This approach requires that both the computer and the device be Bluetooth-enabled.

See Also   For more information about identifying the USB sockets on your mobile PC, see "Identifying Laptop Ports and Jacks" in Chapter 2, "Getting to Know Your Mobile PC Hardware." For details about Bluetooth, see "Using Bluetooth Wireless Technology" in Chapter 3, "Introduction to Networking."

Microsoft provides a program called Microsoft ActiveSync for use with Microsoft *Windows Mobile* and other ActiveSync-compatible devices that make synchronization easy. Note that to use this program, the device must be connected by Bluetooth or through a USB port.

See Also   For more information on ActiveSync, visit *www.microsoft.com/windowsmobile/downloads/default.mspx.*

If your device doesn't support ActiveSync, read the manufacturer's documentation because your device probably includes a manufacturer-specific data synchronization program.

Taking Files Offline by Using Offline Folders

If your mobile PC is part of a network, you probably store some of your files on that network. When you disconnect from the network, you lose access to those files unless you copy them to the hard disk of your mobile PC. Using Windows XP, you can create a copy of files that you want to access offline and that are usually stored on the network. That way, you can continue to read and edit the files, and then copy an updated version onto the network when you reconnect. If someone else changed the file on the network while you were away, you can either save a separate copy of your changed file or overwrite the current file.

Important   Offline files are only available if you're using Windows XP Professional or Window XP Professional Tablet PC Edition.

In this exercise, you will configure your mobile PC to use offline files.

BE SURE TO have access to files and folders stored on a network share before beginning this exercise.

1   Click **Start**, and then click **Control Panel**.

2   In Control Panel, click the **Appearance and Themes** link.

3   In the **Appearance and Themes** window, click the **Folder Options** link.

4   In the **Folder Options** dialog box, click the **Offline Files** tab.

5 Select the **Enable Offline Files** and **Create an Offline Files shortcut on the desktop** check boxes, and then click **OK**.

Note If *Fast User Switching* has been enabled on your mobile PC, these options won't be available. To turn off Fast User Switching, click **Start**, click **Control Panel**, and then click **User Accounts**. In the User Accounts dialog box, click **Change the ways users log on and off**, clear the **Use Fast User Switching** check box, and then click **OK**.

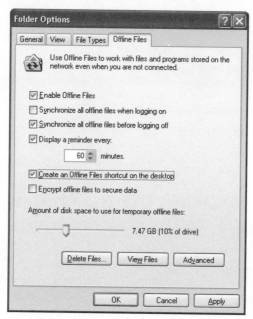

Close

6 In the **Appearance and Themes** window, click the **Close** button.

You are now ready to select the files and folders that you would like to use when you are offline.

7 To specify the files and folders that you want to access offline, click **Start**, and then click **My Network Places**.

8 Right-click the network folder that you want to make available offline, and then click **Make Available Offline**.

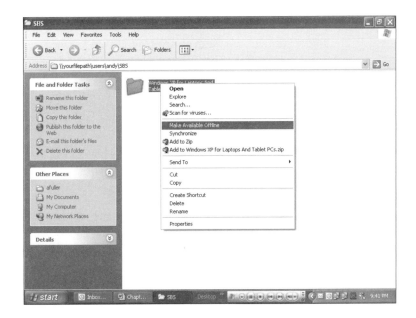

Tip You can also select individual files for offline use by right-clicking on them, and then selecting **Make Available Offline**.

After the synchronization message closes, the folder you originally selected shows an icon identifying that it will be synchronized.

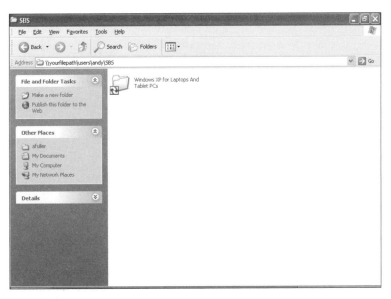

9 In the My Network Places window, click the **Close** button.

10 On the desktop, click the **Shortcut To Offline Files** icon.

This folder contains the files you selected in step 8. While you are connected to the network, you will make changes directly to the files on the network share. When you log off or shutdown, these files synchronize so that you can use them offline.

Tip If you delete a file in the Offline File Folder on your mobile PC, only the local copy is deleted; the original file remains on the network share.

CLOSE the Offline Files Folder window.

Making Web Pages Available Offline

You can also make Web pages available when you are offline. This can be useful if you need information that is only available on an intranet site (such as a list of local phone numbers) when you are traveling, or you just want to be able to browse the content of your favorite Web site while offline.

In this exercise, you will use Internet Explorer to make a Web page available offline.

BE SURE TO have an Internet connection before beginning this exercise.

1 Click **Start**, and then click **Internet Explorer**.

2 In the Address Bar of the Internet Explorer window, type http://www.microsoft.com/security/default.mspx, and then click **Go**.

3 Click the **Favorites** menu, and then click **Add To Favorites**.

4 In the **Add Favorite** dialog box, select the **Make available offline** check box.

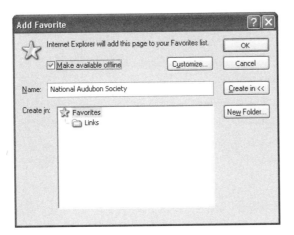

Customize...

Tip   You can also make portions of or entire Web sites available while offline. To do so, in the **Add Favorite** dialog box, click the **Customize** button. On the first page of the Offline Favorite Wizard, click **Next**. On the second page of the wizard, specify how many levels of the Web site (and links to other Web sites) you want to be synchronized. Be aware that the more levels you add, the longer it takes to synchronize when shutting or logging off and the more disk space is required. To manually control when the synchronization occurs, simply click **Synchronize** on the **Tools** menu, or set synchronization to a specific schedule.

5   To start the initial synchronization process, click **OK**.

Important   This might take several minutes, depending on the size of the Web page and the speed of your Internet connection.

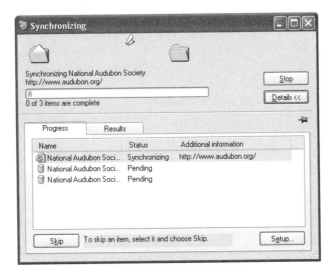

6 In the **Internet Explorer** window, click the **Home** button.

7 Click the **File** menu, and then click **Work Offline**.

You're now disconnected from the Internet and only able to browse pages synchronized to your mobile PC.

8 To verify that you can view the contents of the Audubon Society home page, click the **Favorites** menu, and then click **National Audubon Society**.

9 To find out what happens when you try connecting to a Web page that you have not made available offline, in the **Address Bar**, type www.microsoft.com, and then click **Go**.

The following message appears, giving you the opportunity to try connecting to the Internet.

10 To re-establish your Internet connection, click **Connect**.

CLOSE Internet Explorer.

Accessing E-Mail When Offline

If your company is using Microsoft Exchange Server 2003, you can access your e-mail folders when you are offline by using Microsoft Office Outlook 2003. Outlook 2003 copies your e-mail, calendar, contacts, and tasks to a local cache folder on your mobile PC. This folder is available when you are offline, which allows you to read and edit any of the data it contains. Also, you can compose new e-mails that are sent when you are back online.

See Also To learn more about the offline capabilities of Outlook 2003, visit *office.microsoft.com/outlook/*.

Choosing Useful Items to Carry with You when Away from Your Desk

You have updated your PDA or mobile phone, ensured that your computer has the files, Web pages and e-mails that you want, but you might want to take a few more items with you, especially if you are planning on being away from your desk for a while. You should consider taking the following:

- *Power cord.*   If you think you'll be using the PC for longer than your current battery charge, you should take your power cord and adapter with you.

- *Extra battery.*   If you're going to be somewhere that has no power outlets, you might want to consider taking an extra battery with you (just make sure it is charged before you leave).

- *Mobile PC carrying case.*   If you're traveling, it is probably worth investing in a dedicated, padded carrying case for your mobile PC to make it easier to carry.

If you're going to be traveling for a prolonged period, staying in hotels or traveling internationally, you might also want to consider:

- *Power plug adapter.*   If you're traveling internationally, this is essential.

- *Compact mouse.*   If you will be using your mobile PC for prolonged periods and you find the trackpad uncomfortable to use, you can purchase a special, small mouse that is specifically for mobile PC use.

- *Ethernet cable.*   Many modern hotels provide broadband internet access (sometimes even a wireless network). It is always a good idea to carry an Ethernet cable with you in case there isn't one in the room.

- *Telephone modem cable.*   And, just in case you stay in a hotel without Internet access, you will probably want to have a modem cable as a backup.

Undocking Your Mobile PC

The final step as you leave your desk is to undock your mobile PC from its docking station (assuming you have one).

See Also   For more information about docking stations, see "Understanding Docking Stations and Port Replicators" in Chapter 2, "Getting to Know Your Mobile PC Hardware."

It is important that you undock correctly, as it can cause some issues, such as not shutting off disconnected external devices, if you don't. First, look at your docking station to see if it has a button that you need to press in order to release the computer. If it does, press the button before undocking (refer to the manufacturer's documentation for more details). When you do, it is likely that Windows will go into Standby mode so that it can correctly reconfigure itself.

See Also   For more information about Standby mode, see "Effectively Managing Your Battery" in Chapter 2, "Getting to Know Your Mobile PC Hardware."

If no undock button is available on the docking station, look on the Start or All Programs menu for an Undock button; if one is available, click it before undocking.

If neither type of undock button is available and you are not using extended desktop mode, remove the mobile PC from the docking station and go.

See Also   For more information on extended desktop mode, see "Docking and Using an External Monitor" earlier in this chapter.

If you are using extended desktop mode and no undock button is available, manually turn off extended desktop mode before undocking. To do so:

1   Right-click the desktop, and then click **Properties**.

2   In the **Display Properties** dialog box, click the **Settings** tab.

3   On the **Settings** tab, clear the **Extend my Windows desktop to this monitor** check box, and then click **OK**.

You are now ready to use your mobile PC away from your desk.

Key Points

- You can use your mobile PC in extended desktop mode with an external monitor so that you can be more productive by using both monitors as one large screen.

- You can use instant messaging to quickly send messages and files to co-workers, friends, and family.

- If you have a Tablet PC, you can use the new Tablet PC Input Panel to more efficiently enter and correct text.

- If you have a compatible PDA or mobile phone, you can synchronize information from your computer, such as contact details, calendar appointments, and digital music.

- You can use Offline Files to copy stored network share files to your mobile PC's hard disk files so that you can access them offline.

- You can make Web pages available offline so that you can have access to their content when you are not connected to the Internet.

- Before using your mobile PC away from your desk, you should assess what additional items you need to bring along, based on your destination and the length of your meeting or trip.

- You need to make sure that you undock your mobile PC properly before leaving your desk.

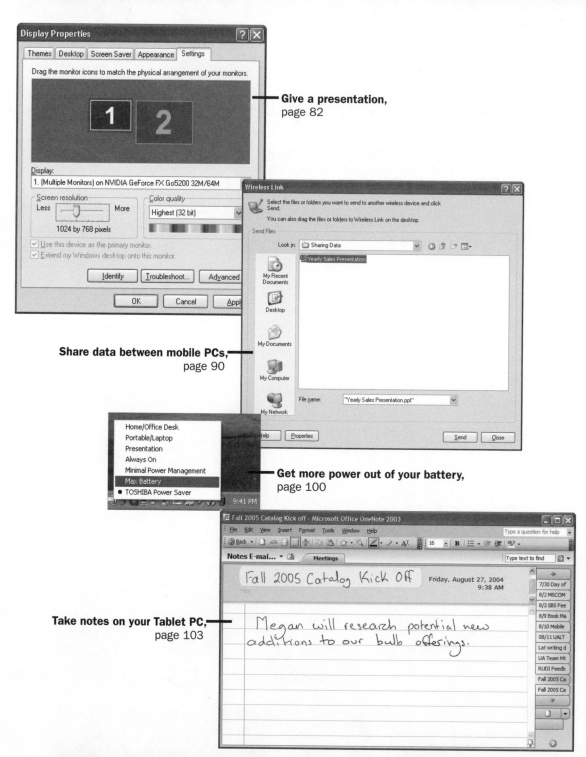

Give a presentation,
page 82

Share data between mobile PCs,
page 90

Get more power out of your battery,
page 100

Take notes on your Tablet PC,
page 103

Chapter 5 at a Glance

5 Using Your Mobile PC in Meetings

In this chapter you will learn to:

✔   Give a presentation.

✔   Share data between mobile PCs.

✔   Get more power out of your battery.

✔   Take notes on your Tablet PC.

The use of wireless networks has been increasing over the past couple of years, particularly in busy offices, in coffee shops, and on university campuses. If you use a mobile PC while in the office, wireless networks make it easier for you to work away from your desk and to use your mobile computer in more places.

In the workplace, mobile PCs are particularly useful at meetings. You can use your mobile PC to display Microsoft PowerPoint or other electronic presentations, share information with other mobile PC users over a network, and efficiently record and distribute meeting notes.

Important   The corporate culture of some companies doesn't permit the use of mobile PCs in meetings for fear that the mobile PC will detract the attendees' focus from the meeting.

It is not uncommon for meeting organizers to want to share documents with the meeting participants (for example, to distribute a copy of the presentation). You will often see people passing out printed copies of presentation materials, rather than taking advantage of their mobile PCs to share files.

In this chapter, you will learn how to use Microsoft Windows XP to project a presentation in a more professional way, share documents with other mobile PC users, optimize your power settings to get the most power out of your PC's battery, and take meeting notes.

See Also   Do you need only a quick refresher on the topics in this chapter? See the Quick Reference entries on pages xxv–xxix.

 Important   Before you can use the practice files in this chapter, you need to install them from the book's companion CD to their default location. See "Using the Book's CD-ROM" on page xiii for more information.

Giving a Presentation

If you use a mobile PC in meetings, chances are that you've displayed documents, such as agendas, from your mobile PC, or perhaps even given presentations. The most common way to give a presentation from your mobile PC is to use a projector to display content from your mobile PC on a projector screen.

The purpose of this section is not to describe how to give a good presentation using PowerPoint, but rather to give you some tips on how to set up your mobile PC to optimize the quality and professionalism of your presentations.

You connect your mobile PC to a projector by using a VGA cable—the same type of cable you use to connect your mobile PC to a desktop monitor. Take a look at the various sockets on the back or side of your mobile PC and locate the VGA socket resembling the one shown in the illustration below.

See Also   For more information about identifying the sockets on your mobile PC, refer to "Identifying the Ports and Jacks on your Laptop" in Chapter 2, "Getting to Know Your Mobile PC Hardware."

Tip   Projector cables can suffer a lot of wear and tear from daily use. When plugging the cable into your PC, make sure it is a pressed firmly into place. If it is loose, consider tightening the two screws on the connector.

You can display your mobile PC content through a projector in two modes:

■   You can use *mirrored mode* (sometimes referred to as *cloned mode*) to duplicate your mobile PC screen on the projector screen. In this mode, you will know with certainty that what you are seeing on your screen is what your audience is seeing. The downside of using this mode is that instant messaging pop-ups, e-mail notifications, and other potentially irritating messages can appear on the screen, interrupting your presentation. Also, if you move between programs (for example, to show a spreadsheet), the audience will be watching your actions, and will see your desktop background and icons. This can give a rather unpolished feel to your presentation.

■ You can use *extended desktop mode* (also called *DualView*) to extend Windows and use two (or more) displays together as one large display. You can then project your presentation and use your mobile PC screen independently. This mode gives the presentation a more polished look by addressing the two main drawbacks of mirrored mode, and allows you to do something else during the presentation, such as take notes.

Projecting a Presentation by Using Mirrored Mode

The steps to follow to give a presentation in mirrored mode depend on the hardware and software settings defined by the manufacturer of your mobile PC. Most mobile PC screens can be toggled to mirrored mode either by clicking an icon in the notification area or by pressing a function key combination (often either FUNCTION+F5 or FUNCTION+F8). The function key to use might be labeled with a monitor icon, or with the phrase CRT/LCD. If you can't locate the screen toggle command, you will need to refer to the PC manufacturer's documentation.

Important   No two PC manufacturers implement the screen toggle functionality in quite the same way. Some screen toggle buttons toggle mirroring on and off, while others throw extended desktop into the mix—you'll need to experiment with your mobile PC and a projector or desktop monitor to determine how your screen toggle function works.

If you're unable to identify a function key or are using either a slate Tablet PC or a convertible Tablet PC as a slate, you'll need to use a program to switch to mirrored mode. Usually, you'll find that program in the *notification area* (the area at the far right of the Windows taskbar). The program is usually represented by an icon that looks like a monitor. Right-click that icon and look for the *mirrored mode* (or *cloned mode*) option on the shortcut menu.

Troubleshooting Your Presentation in Mirrored Mode

After you have enabled mirrored mode on the mobile PC, you should see a duplicate image of your mobile PC screen on the projector screen. It is not uncommon, however, to run into problems when switching to mirrored mode.

If the image is not displaying correctly on the projector screen, right-click the desktop, and then click Properties. In the Display Properties dialog box, click the Settings tab, and then try one of the following:

Problem	Solution	Additional information
There is no image at all on the projector screen. -or- There is a flickering image on the projector screen.	Decrease the screen resolution of the mobile PC by dragging the **Screen resolution** slider to the left (to either 1024×768 or 800×600), and then clicking **OK**.	The cause of this problem is an incompatibility between what the mobile PC is sending to the projector and what the projector is capable of receiving.
There is an image on the projector screen, but it is partially off of the screen and you have a laptop with a widescreen.	Switch to a screen resolution that uses a different aspect ratio by dragging the **Screen resolution** slider to the left (to one of the following: 1280×1024, 1024×768 or 800×600), and then clicking **OK**.	Many new laptop designs, particularly those aimed at the consumer market, have a wide aspect ratio screen (often 16:10) whereas a projector often only supports the conventional TV and monitor shape and aspect ratio (4:3).
The image on the projector screen is on its side (and you're using a Tablet PC).	Adjust the screen orientation of your Tablet PC by tapping on the **Change tablet and pen settings** icon in the notification area, and then clicking **Change screen orientation** as many times as necessary to correct the screen orientation.	Tablet PCs have a hardware button that can be used to change the screen orientation. Refer to the manufacturer's documentation to identify which button controls the screen orientation.

Projecting a Presentation by Using Extended Desktop Mode

You can use *extended desktop* mode with a meeting room projector to give your presentation a more polished look. This mode gives you tighter control of what the audience gets to see, as well as the ability to perform other actions on your computer, such as take notes.

Setting Up for Extended Desktop Mode

Before you can start a presentation using the extended desktop mode you have to configure your mobile PC to use it.

In this exercise, you will configure your mobile PC to use the extended desktop mode.

BE SURE TO connect the projector cable to the VGA port on the back of your computer before beginning this exercise.

1   Right-click the desktop, and then click **Properties**.

The Display Properties dialog box appears.

2   In the **Display Properties** dialog box, click the **Settings** tab.

Note that there are two blue rectangles representing your displays and that Monitor 2 is unavailable because it hasn't yet been enabled.

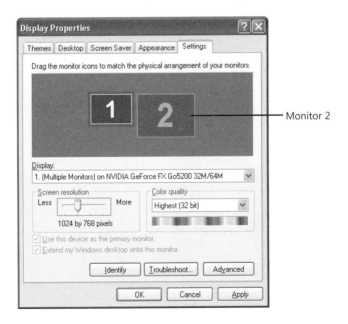

3 To enable Monitor 2, click the visual representation of Monitor 2, select the **Extend my Windows desktop onto this monitor** check box, and then click **OK**.

The following message box appears and gives you 15 seconds to confirm that the new mode you have selected is working correctly, otherwise it will revert to the previous mode.

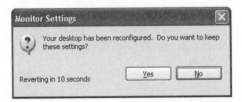

4 If an image of your desktop background is showing on the projector screen while your mobile PC screen continues to show not only your desktop background, but also your taskbar, any open programs, icons, and so on, click **Yes**.

Your mobile PC is now configured for extended desktop mode.

Troubleshooting   If the image on the projector screen is flickering or rotated, refer to the instructions in *Troubleshooting Your Presentation in Mirrored Mode* earlier in this chapter.

Adjusting the Monitor Positions

By default, Windows places the second screen (in this case, the projector) to the right of the first one. The two separate screens work like one large desktop. For example, if you move the mouse to the right while you are on Monitor 1, your cursor moves to Monitor 2. Just as you can move your cursor between screens, you can drag icons and programs between Monitors 1 and 2.

You can also change the position of Monitor 2 to better reflect the physical position of the screen in the conference room. For example, if the projector screen is to your left, it might be easier to have the projector screen configured as Monitor 1 so you can scroll left with the mouse.

In this exercise, you will change the position of Monitor 2 to better reflect its physical position.

1 Right-click the desktop, and then click **Properties**.

2 In the **Display Properties** dialog box, click the **Settings** tab.

3 Drag the graphical representation of Monitor 2 (the blue box with the 2 in it) to the left of Monitor 1, and then click **OK**.

Tip   If you lose track of which screen is which, right-click the desktop, click **Properties**, click the **Settings** tab in the **Display Properties** dialog box, and then click **Identify**.

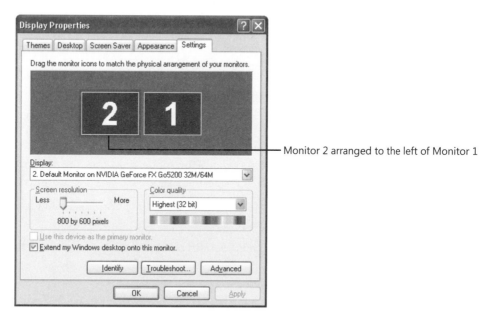

Monitor 2 arranged to the left of Monitor 1

4   The following message box appears and gives you 15 seconds to confirm that the new mode you have selected is working correctly, otherwise it will revert to the previous mode.

Moving Programs to the Second Monitor

You can place any programs you wish to use during a presentation onto the projector screen by starting the program the way you normally do, and then dragging it to the other screen.

In this exercise, you will move the Microsoft Internet Explorer program to the other monitor.

1   Click **Start**, and then click **Internet Explorer**.

Internet Explorer opens on your mobile PC screen.

2 Drag the Internet Explorer window to the second monitor.

Troubleshooting If you cannot drag the Internet Explorer window, it might be because the window is maximized. To fix the problem, click the **Restore Down** button on the title bar of the window, and then try dragging it again.

Maximize

3 To make the Internet Explorer window fill the projector screen, click the **Maximize** button on the title bar of the window.

Tip It is often easier to press [Alt]+[Tab] to switch between programs that are on the extended desktop than it is to scroll between displays.

Close

4 Click the **Close** button on Internet Explorer.

5 To stop using extended desktop mode, right-click the desktop, click **Properties**, and then in the **Display Properties** dialog box, click the **Settings** tab.

6 On the **Settings** tab, clear the **Extend my Windows desktop onto this monitor** check box, and then click **OK**.

Note that any open programs on Monitor 2 are now moved back to your mobile PC screen.

Using Microsoft PowerPoint Presenter View

If you create and deliver your presentations using PowerPoint 2002 or later, you can take advantage of a built-in tool, Presenter View, to have more control over the slide show. With this tool, you, as the presenter, will be able to advance slides and read speaker notes on your mobile PC screen while the slide deck is shown on the projector screen.

In this exercise, you will show a presentation using the PowerPoint Presenter View.

BE SURE TO install PowerPoint 2002 or later, connect your mobile PC to the projector, and turn on extended desktop view before beginning this exercise.
USE the *Yearly Sales Presentation* slideshow in the practice file folder for this topic. This practice file is located in the *My Documents\Microsoft Press\Laptops and Tablet PCs with Windows XP SBS \Presentations\UsingPresenter* folder.

1 Click **Start**, point to **All Programs**, point to **Microsoft Office**, and then click **Microsoft PowerPoint**.

2 On the **Slide Show** menu, click **Set Up Show**.

3   In the **Set Up Show** dialog box, select the **Show Presenter View** check box, and then click **OK**.

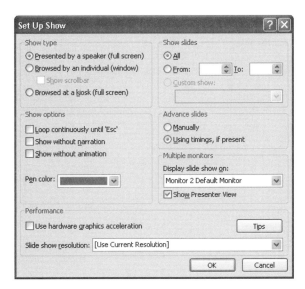

4   On the **File** menu, click **Open**.

The Open dialog box appears.

5   In the **Name** box of the **Open** dialog box, double-click the **My Documents** folder, the **Microsoft Press** folder, the **Laptops and Tablet PCs with Windows XP SBS** folder, the **Presentations** folder, the **UsingPresenter** folder, and then double-click **Yearly Sales Presentation**.

Note that the presentation opens automatically in Presenter View on your ***primary*** display (which should be your mobile PC screen).

Tip   Keyboard shortcut keys can be a great asset when giving a presentation. For example, you can move through slides in PowerPoint by using the ← and → keys on the numeric keypad.

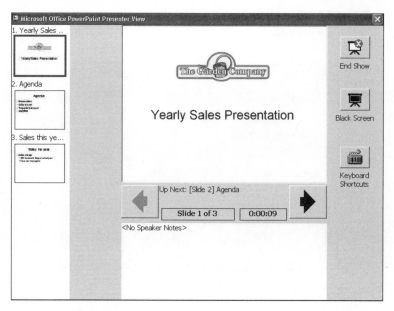

Close

6 When you have finished the presentation, on the PowerPoint window title bar, click the **Close** button.

You are returned to your standard Windows desktop.

7 To stop using extended desktop mode, right-click the desktop, click **Properties**, and then in the **Display Properties** dialog box, click the **Settings** tab.

8 On the **Settings** tab, clear the **Extend my Windows desktop onto this monitor** check box, and then click **OK**.

BE SURE TO complete steps 7 and 8 so that Windows is aware that you have disconnected your mobile PC from the projector; otherwise programs might remain open on Monitor 2, where they will not be visible.

Sharing Data Between Mobile PCs

When using your mobile away from your office and in a collaborative environment, you often need to or want to share data with others around you. For example, if you are giving a presentation to a group of colleagues or clients, you may want to share a copy of the PowerPoint presentation with them so that they can refer to their own copy during the meeting or take notes on the slides if they're using a Tablet PC.

Until recently, the easiest way to share documents while on the go was for people to provide a floppy disk with the relevant data. As size and portability become paramount for mobile PCs, most now don't come with a floppy disk drive. However, there are at least three ways to quickly share data without the help of a trusty floppy disk.

Tip An easy way to share your contact data with other people is by sending them a vCard, an electronic business card that the recipient can save to his or her contacts list. The vCard standard was created by the Internet Mail Consortium and is supported by all major e-mail programs. To create your own vCard in Microsoft Office Outlook 2003, on the **File** menu, point to **New**, and then click **Contact**. In the Untitled – Contact window, enter your contact information. On the **File** menu, click **Export to vCard** file, type a name in the **File name** box, and then click **Save**.

Sharing Data by Using a USB Flash Drive

The USB flash drive is the floppy disk of the 21st century. It is a small data storage device, barely bigger than a key chain, that you can plug into the USB port of any computer. Windows XP recognizes the USB flash drive as a removable storage device, like a mini disk drive. USB flash drives are available from most computer peripheral retailers.

In this exercise, you will use a USB flash drive to quickly and reliably move data between mobile PCs.

BE SURE TO have a USB flash drive available before beginning this exercise.

1 Plug the USB flash drive into an available USB port.

After a few seconds an audio chime sounds and a notification appears, notifying you that the hardware has been recognized and is now configured.

> **Found New Hardware** ✕
> USB Mass Storage Device

2 Click **Start**, and then click **My Computer**.

Note that a new drive is now listed in the Devices with Removable Storage area.

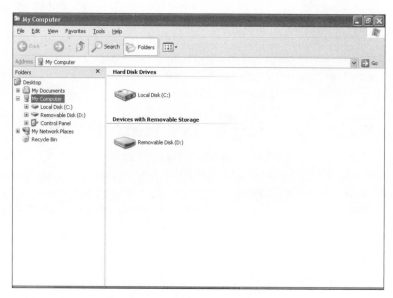

3 In the **My Computer** folder, double-click the **USB Drive** icon to display a list of the files stored on the drive.

You can then use the files like you would with files stored on any other storage device.

Tip USB flash drives are limited by the amount of memory on the device, but they are usually adequate for sharing data (for example, presentations, documents, or spreadsheets) in most casual collaborative environments.

4 Remove the USB flash drive from the USB port.

5 On the title bar of the **My Computer** window, click the **Close** button.

The My Computer window closes.

Close

Sharing Data by Using Infrared Data Transmission

Another efficient way to share data with others is to take advantage of infrared data transmission. The majority of mobile PCs support transmission of data to other PCs and devices using infrared. The Infrared Data Association (IrDA) has defined a standard for data transmission between devices. IrDA is short-range (usually less than 3 feet), has a slow transfer rate, and can be a little tricky to use because the two PCs need to be perfectly aligned for the data transfer to work reliably. But since most mobile PCs support this data transfer method, you can usually rely on it to share files with others.

Not every mobile PC has infrared capabilities. To check your mobile PC, take a look at the bezel of your PC for a rectangle of dark red plastic approximately one half inch across "flanked" by a helpful icon.

In this exercise, you will check the availability of infrared on your computer and send files to another PC using infrared data transmission.

BE SURE TO to have a second mobile PC with infrared data transmission capabilities available before beginning this exercise.

1　Click **Start**, right-click **My Computer**, and then click **Properties**.

The Systems Properties dialog box appears.

2　In the **Systems Properties** dialog box, click the **Hardware** tab, and then click **Device Manager**.

The Device Manager window appears.

3　In the Device Manager window, scroll down the list until you locate the **Infrared devices** section.

If the "Infrared devices" section does not appear in the list, your PC does not support infrared data transmission.

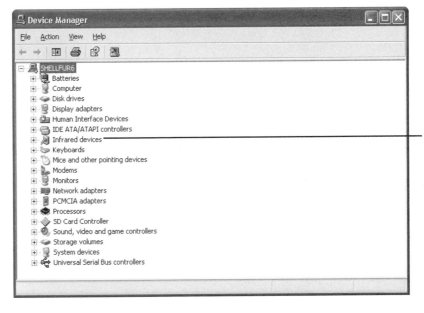

If your PC has any infrared devices, they will appear here.

4 Confirm that the person with whom you want to share files also has a mobile PC that supports IrDA by following the steps above for that computer. Once it has been confirmed, continue with the following steps.

5 Place the two computers within 3 feet of each other, and make sure that the infrared ports are facing each other.

After a few seconds, a notification appears on both computers, notifying you that there is another PC nearby, and the **Wireless Link** icon should appear in the notification area.

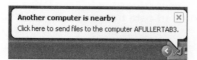

Another computer is nearby [×]
Click here to send files to the computer AFULLERTAB3.

6 After the connection between the computers has been established, in the notification area, double-click the **Wireless Link** icon.

The Wireless Link dialog box appears.

7 In the **Wireless Link** dialog box, select the files you want to share, and then click **Send**.

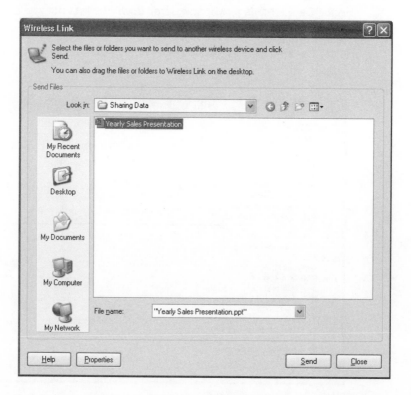

8 When a message box appears on the second PC notifying you that files have been sent and are available for download, click **Yes** to start the file transfer process.

9 To terminate the connection, move the PCs so that the infrared ports do not point at each other.

Important   The data that is sent over the infrared link is not encrypted. If you are concerned about security, make sure the two PCs are very close to one another so that the data is not unintentionally available to other nearby PCs or devices.

Creating an Ad Hoc Wireless Network to Share Data

If you use your mobile PC to connect to the Internet or any other networks, you are probably familiar with establishing and using wireless connections. You can also configure PCs to connect directly to one another by creating an *ad hoc wireless network*—your very own mini network. This is particularly useful if you are not in range of an infrastructure wireless network, and want to share information, for example, to share files with a group of people you meet at a conference.

Using Windows XP, you can configure a secure ad hoc wireless network by either using the Wireless Setup Wizard or using a USB flash drive to transfer the configuration data between the mobile PCs.

In this exercise, you will create and use a wireless network to share files between PCs.

BE SURE TO disconnect from all wired or wireless networks and have a USB flash drive and a second mobile PC running Windows XP Service Pack 2 (SP2) or later available before beginning this exercise.
USE the *Yearly Sales Presentation* PowerPoint presentation in the practice file folder for this topic. These practice files are located in the *My Documents\Microsoft Press\Laptops and Tablet PCs with Windows XP SBS\Presentations\SharingData* folder.

1 Click **Start**, and then click **Control Panel**.

2 In Control Panel, click the **Network and Internet Connections** link.

3 In the Network and Internet Connections window, click **Network Connections**.

4 In the Network Connections window, right-click the **Wireless Network Connection** icon, and then click **View Available Wireless Network**.

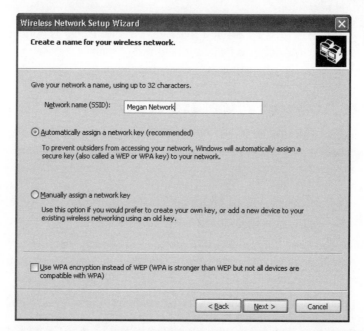

Important If you are connected to another wireless network, click the network in the list, and then click the **Disconnect** button.

5 In the **Network Tasks** area of the **Wireless Network Connection** dialog box, click the **Set up a wireless network** link.

6 On the first page of the Wireless Network Setup Wizard, click **Next**.

7 On the **Choose a key for your wireless network** page, enter a name for the network and click **Next**.

8 On the **Choose a method for setting up your wireless network** page, click **Next** (since this list of steps assumes that you are using a USB flash drive).

9 Insert the USB flash drive into the USB port of your mobile PC, and then on the **Save settings to your flash drive** page, click **Next**.

After a few seconds, the ad hoc wireless network configuration settings will be copied to your USB flash drive.

10 Unplug the USB flash drive and plug it into the PC you want to add to your network.

After the PC finishes reading the configuration settings from the USB flash drive, a list of options is displayed in the Removable Disk (D:) dialog box.

11 In the **What do you want Windows to do?** area, click **Wireless Network Setup Wizard**, and then click **OK**.

12 When prompted to confirm the addition of the PC to the new ad hoc wireless network, click **OK**.

Repeat steps 10 through 12 for each PC you want to add to the network, up to a maximum of 16.

13 Click **Start**, and then click **My Documents**.

14 In the My Documents window, browse to the *Microsoft Press\Laptops and Tablet PCs with Windows XP SBS\Presentations\SharingData* folder.

The contents of the SharingData folder are displayed.

15 On the **File and Folder Tasks** menu, click **Share This Folder**.

16 In the **My Shared Files Properties** dialog box, click the **Sharing** tab, click the **Share This Folder** option, and then click **OK**.

The hand below the folder indicates that the folder is now being shared.

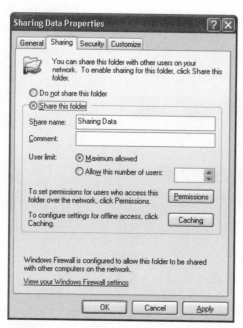

17 To find the name of the computer on which the shared data is stored, click **Start**, right-click **My Computer**, and then click **Properties**.

The System Properties dialog box appears.

18 In the **System Properties** dialog box, click the **Computer Name** tab.

The name of the computer is displayed to the right of **Full computer name**.

Important   If your PC is part of a corporate domain, you can find the domain name to the right of **Domain**. If you look to the right of **Full computer name**, you will see your computer name with the domain name appended to it. You need only the computer name for this exercise.

19   On the taskbar of one of the PCs that you added to the ad hoc network, click **Start**, and then click **My Network Places**.

The My Network Places window appears.

Go

20   In the Address Bar, type \\ followed by the name of the computer that is hosting the shared content, and then click the **Go** button.

The PC will search the ad hoc network to find the other PC. This may take a few seconds.

21   When the other PC is successfully located, on the updated My Network Places page, double-click the **Sharing Data** folder.

You can now open any of the files in the Sharing Data folder, or copy them to the PC to use later.

Close

22 On the title bar of the My Network Places window, click the **Close** button.

Getting More Power Out of Your Battery

If you've used your mobile PC to give a presentation or take notes in an environment that required you to run the computer strictly on battery, you've probably worried about running out of power before completing the task. One of the most common ways to relieve the anxiety is to lug around an extra battery, or take your power cord with you in hope that a power socket will be available in case of emergency.

You might have also watched in dismay as your PC screen turns black after a couple of minutes, forcing you to wiggle the mouse to "wake" your computer up. By turning off your screen, Windows is trying to help you maximize your battery life since the screen is the largest draw on the battery in the PC. However well-intentioned, this type of automatic action can be frustrating.

Windows XP offers several power schemes that you can configure to ensure your mobile PC behaves the way you want.

If you are planning to give a presentation and want to ensure that your computer screen is up and running at all times, you can modify the selected power scheme to prevent it from turning off.

In this exercise, you will modify power options to ensure that your computer screen never turns off.

1 Click **Start**, and then click **Control Panel**.

2 In Control Panel, click **Performance and Maintenance**.

3 In the Performance and Maintenance window, click **Power Options**.

4   On the **Power Schemes** tab of the **Power Options Properties** dialog box, click the **Power schemes** arrow and then click **Presentation** in the drop-down list.

The **Turn off monitor** option is now set to **Never** when running on batteries.

Note   If you want to adjust the length of time before the system goes into standby while on batteries, you can change that value on the **Power Schemes** tab of the **Power Options Properties** dialog box.

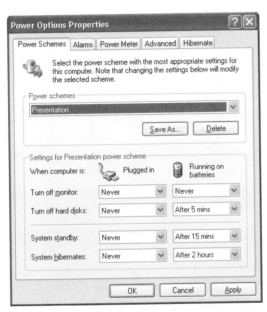

5   To apply and use the **Presentation** power scheme, click **OK**.

6   When you have finished the presentation, in the notification area, right-click the battery meter icon, and then click **Adjust Power Options**.

7   On the **Power Schemes** tab of the **Power Options Properties** dialog box, click the **Power schemes** arrow and click **Portable/Laptop** in the list.

Power settings to maximize your battery life are now applied.

Optimizing Battery Life

To get the longest possible battery life while attending the meeting, click the battery meter in the notification area, and then click **Max Battery**. The Max Battery power scheme is designed to conserve as much power as possible and will cause the screen to go black frequently.

If you're using a Tablet PC, you can dim the screen brightness to optimize battery life. Turning down screen brightness will save battery power and is worth considering, but you will want to experiment with the settings and identify the lowest level you are comfortable with.

Follow these steps to adjust the screen brightness setting to lessen power consumption.

1   In the notification area, double-tap the **Change tablet and pen settings** icon.

2   In the **Tablet and Pen Settings** dialog box, click the **Display** tab.

3   In the **Screen Brightness** area, click the down arrow to the right of the **Settings for** button, and then click **Powered by batteries**.

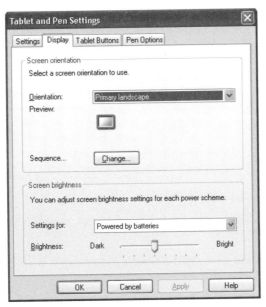

4   Move the **Brightness** slider to the left to dim the screen and lessen the power on the battery, and then click **OK**.

5   On the title bar of the **Tablet and Pen Settings** dialog box, click **Close**.

Close

Taking Notes on Your Tablet PC

If you're a meeting attendee rather than a presenter, there is a good chance that you'll want to jot down notes (or just doodle!). Instead of hand writing on a notepad, you can use your Tablet PC.

Taking notes on your Tablet PC has a couple of key advantages over using paper:

■   It is easier to manage and archive notes in a single location.

■   It is easier to share notes with other people.

Some of the key features of Microsoft OneNote are:

■   You can organize notes into Sections.

■   You can flag a note so that you can identify it quickly later.

■   You can convert notes into Outlook tasks.

In this exercise you will take notes on your Tablet PC by using Microsoft Office OneNote 2003 Service Pack 1 (SP1), create an Outlook task from your notes, and annotate a screen clipping.

BE SURE TO install Microsoft Office OneNote 2003 SP1 or later and Microsoft Office Outlook 2003 or later before beginning this exercise.
USE the *Fall 2005 Catalog Layout* note in the practice file folder for this topic. This practice file is located in the *My Documents\Microsoft Press\Laptops and Tablet PCs with Windows XP SBS \Presentations\TakingNotes* folder.

> **Tip** The latest updates for Microsoft OneNote are available from *office.microsoft.com /officeupdate/*.

1 Tap **Start**, tap **All Programs**, tap **Microsoft Office**, and then tap **Microsoft OneNote 2003**.

2 In the **Section Tabs** area, tap the **Meetings** tab.

3 On the right side of the note page, tap the **New Page** icon to create a page.

4 In the **Title** box at the top of the page, using your Tablet PC pen, write Fall 2005 Catalog Kick Off.

5 In the body of the page, write Megan will research potential new additions to our bulb offerings.

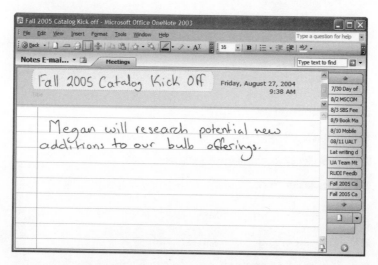

6 To open a page that contains notes from another meeting, browse to the *My Documents\Microsoft Press\Laptops and Tablet PCs with Windows XP SBS \Presentations\TakingNotes* folder, and then tap **Fall 2005 Catalog Layout**.

7 To add a page so that you can add more notes, in the lower-right corner of the page, tap the **Page Down** icon.

8   To flag part of the note as an important issue to follow up on, select **Confirm with Mike Galos that rates have been negotiated with Dutch nursery**, tap the **Note Flag** arrow, and then tap **Important** in the menu.

A yellow star now appears next to the selected text.

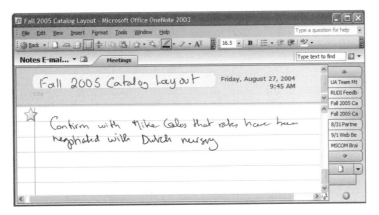

9   To convert an action item into a task that you can track using Outlook, select **Coordinate bulb inventory with Catherine**.

10   On the **Format** menu, tap **Note Flags**, and then tap **Create Outlook Task**.

A Task window opens and the handwritten text you selected in the note is converted to text and entered in the **Subject** box on the **Task** tab.

11   To add the task to your list of Outlook tasks, click the **Save and Close** button.

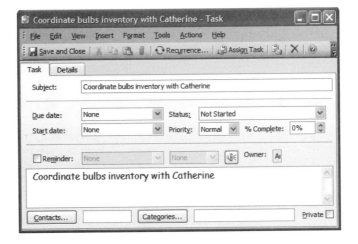

Tip You can also turn your notes into an Outlook Appointment or Contact directly from OneNote. To do this, highlight some text, click the **Tools** menu, point to **Create an Outlook Item**, and then click the appropriate Outlook item on the menu.

12 To select an area of screen to insert into your notes, click the **Insert** menu, and then click **Screen Clipping**.

OneNote automatically minimizes and the screen clipping tool takes over the desktop.

13 Holding down the tablet pen button, drag to select the area of the screen that you wish to capture and to include in your note.

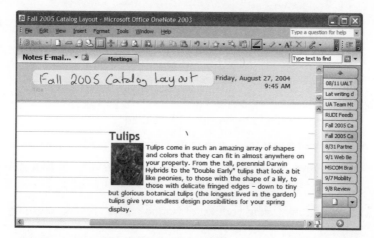

When you release the tablet pen button, the clipped area of screen will automatically be copied into OneNote.

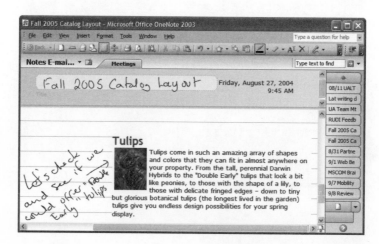

You can now annotate the screen clipping using your pen.

Close

14 To close OneNote, click the **Close** button on the title bar of the OneNote window.

Taking Notes by Using Windows Journal

You can also use Windows Journal, an accessory included as part of Windows XP Tablet PC Edition, to take notes.

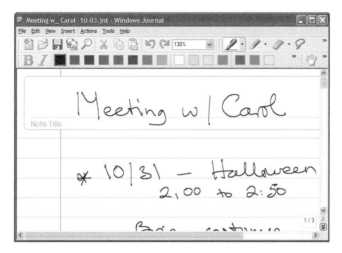

Windows Journal enables you, among other things, to:

■ Flip between pages, as you would in a paper notebook, by either pressing the up and down icons in the lower-right corner of the page, or by pressing the [Page Up] and [Page Down] keys.

■ Customize the size and color of ink you write with.

Highlighter

■ Highlight part of the page using the **Highlighter** button on the **Pen** toolbar.

Flag

■ Flag lines of text with different markers using the **Flag** button on the **Pen** toolbar.

Eraser

■ Correct any errors using the **Eraser** button on the **Pen** toolbar.

■ Import files (such as Microsoft Word documents) and annotate them by tapping the **File** menu, tapping **Import**, and then browsing to and tapping the file you wish to import.

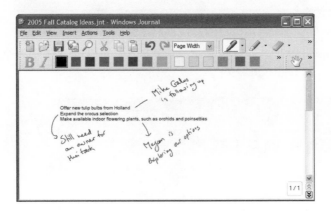

Key Points

- You can project the contents of your mobile PC screen to a second screen by using either mirrored mode or extended desktop mode.

- When using the extended desktop mode, you can take notes on your mobile PC while showing a presentation on the projector.

- You can share data with other mobile PC users in a meeting by using infrared transmission, a USB flash drive, or even an ad hoc wireless network.

- You can increase the life of your mobile PC battery by optimizing the PC's power usage.

- You can be more efficient in meetings by using either OneNote 2003 or Windows Journal to take ink notes on your Tablet PC.

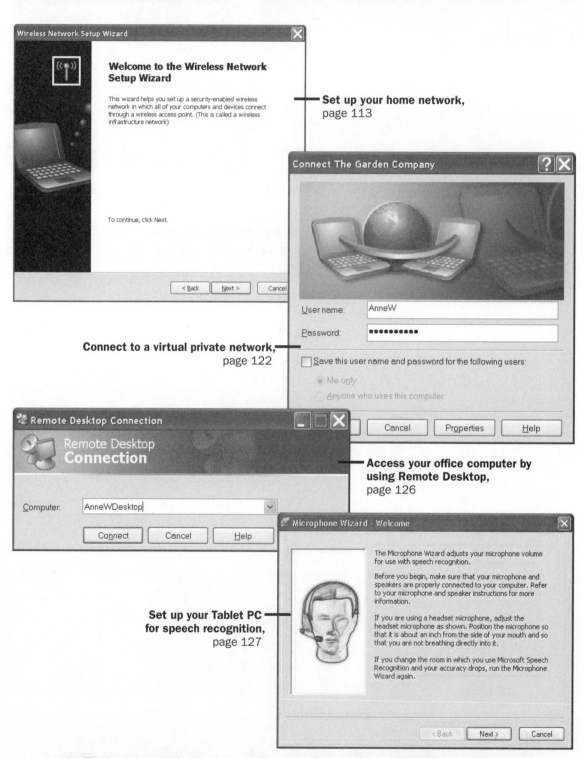

Set up your home network, page 113

Connect to a virtual private network, page 122

Access your office computer by using Remote Desktop, page 126

Set up your Tablet PC for speech recognition, page 127

Chapter 6 at a Glance

6 Using Your Mobile PC at Home

In this chapter you will learn to:

✔ Assign a name and description to your computer.

✔ Set up your home network.

✔ Share an Internet connection.

✔ Share a printer.

✔ Share a network folder.

✔ Move data between computers.

✔ Connect to a virtual private network.

✔ Access your office computer by using Remote Desktop.

✔ Set up your Tablet PC for speech recognition.

As mobile PCs become more prevalent in the work place, many people take them home at the end of the day, either to catch up on e-mail or to work remotely.

In this chapter, you will learn how to assign a name and description to your computer and set up a home network. You will also learn how to share an Internet connection, printer, or network folder, and move data between computers. You will learn how to connect to your organization's network, as well as connect to your office computer by using Remote Desktop. If you have a Tablet PC, you will learn how to take advantage of the Speech Recognition functionality of Microsoft Windows XP to create a document while you are sitting comfortably on your sofa or at your desk.

See Also   Do you need only a quick refresher on the topics in this chapter? See the Quick Reference entries on pages xxix–xxxiii.

Important   Before you can use the practice files in this chapter, you need to install them from the book's companion CD to their default location. See "Using the Book's CD-ROM" on page xiii for more information.

Assigning a Name and Description to Your Computer

Every computer has a unique name to identify it on a domain or in a workgroup. When naming a computer, you can also provide a description to explicitly reflect its location or usage so that it can be easily identified.

In this exercise, you will provide a description for your mobile PC and change its name.

BE SURE TO log on as an administrator or as a member of the Administrators group before beginning this exercise.

> **Troubleshooting** If your computer is connected to a network, network policy settings might prevent you from completing the steps below. Contact your system administrator for more details.

1 Click **Start**, right-click **My Computer**, and then click **Properties**.

2 In the **System Properties** dialog box, click the **Computer Name** tab.

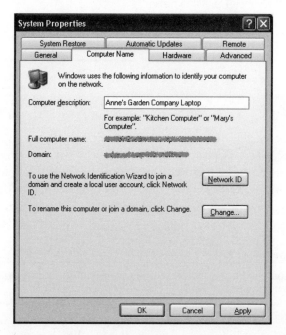

3 In the **Computer description** box, type Anne's Work Laptop.

4 To modify the computer name, click **Change**.

5 In the **Computer Name Changes** dialog box, type AnneW02.

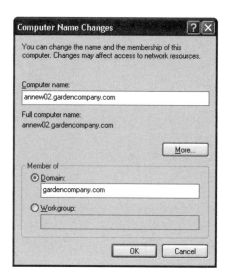

6   To close the open dialog boxes and not apply the changes, click **Cancel** twice.

Important   If your computer is a member of a workgroup, has no networking protocols available, or does not have TCP/IP installed, the computer name must be 15 or fewer
characters long, and all the characters must be uppercase. For example, the sample
computer name used in this exercise would be ANNEW02. Regardless of the case in which
you enter the name, Windows XP converts it to uppercase.

Setting Up Your Home Network

If you have more than one computer, you can create a network to share printers, files,
folders, and even an Internet connection. With a home network, people in your house-
hold can work on different computers at the same time, while still sharing common
resources. For example, you can check e-mail on your mobile PC while your teenage
son surfs the Internet on your family's desktop computer to find information for a history
report.

There are several ways to connect computers or to create a network. In a home environment, the most common model is through a workgroup. Computers directly communicate with each other and do not require a server to manage network resources. Each
workgroup user specifies the data that is shared with and available to other network
users on his or her computer. By sharing common resources, users can print from a
single printer, access information in shared folders, and work on a single instance
of a file without having to create multiple versions of the file or transfer the file between
computers.

By creating and using a home network, you can do any of the following:

■   Use one computer to secure your entire network and protect your Internet
connection.

■ Share one Internet connection with all of the computers on the network.

■ Work on shared files stored on any network computer.

■ Share printers with all of the computers on the network.

In this exercise, you will set up a wireless home network.

BE SURE TO have a wireless access point and USB flash drive available before beginning this exercise.

1 Click **Start**, and then click **Control Panel**.

2 In Control Panel, click the **Network and Internet Connections** link.

3 In the **Network and Internet Connections** window, click **Set up a wireless network for a home or small office**.

The Wireless Network Setup Wizard starts.

4 On the wizard's first page, click **Next**.

The "Create a name for your wireless network" page appears.

5 In the **Network name (SSID)** box, type The Wallace Wireless Network, make sure that the **Automatically assign a network key (recommended)** option is selected, and then click **Next**.

6 On the **How do you want to setup your network?** page, select the **Use a USB flash drive** option, and then click **Next**.

7 Plug your USB flash drive into your USB port, click the USB flash drive in the **Flash drive** drop-down list, and then click **Next**.

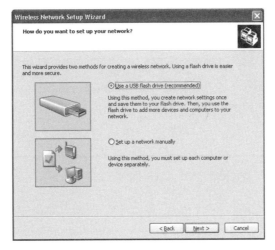

8 Remove the USB flash drive from your mobile PC's USB port, and plug it into your wireless access point.

9 Plug in the USB flash drive in each of the computers you want to join the home network.

10 When you are done, plug the USB flash drive back into the mobile PC you started the process on, and then click **Next**.

11 Click **Finish**.

Sharing an Internet Connection

You can set up one computer to share an Internet connection with the rest of the computers on your home network. This computer is called the Internet Connection Sharing (ICS) host computer. By using ICS, all the members of your family can be connected to the Internet at the same time through a single connection point.

Use the following guidelines to determine which computer should be the ICS host computer:

■ The computer should be running Windows XP.

■ The computer must be one that you can leave on at all times to ensure a continuous Internet connection for all network computers.

■ If one computer has a DSL or cable modem, use that computer as the ICS host computer.

If you plan to use a shared network printer, connect the printer to the ICS host computer.

Troubleshooting If Internet Connection Sharing is already set up on another network computer, be sure to disable ICS on that computer before enabling it on the new host computer.

Sharing a Printer

You can take full advantage of a home network by sharing resources such as a printer. When you are contemplating sharing a printer, consider the following issues:

■ Place the network printer in a central location so that it is convenient for everyone on the network.

■ Distance is an important issue when using a network printer with a mobile PC; beyond 15 feet, the signals fade and the ability to print can be compromised.

■ If your printer is not connected to your home network, you can connect it to multiple computers by using a printer switch. There are two types of switches: manual and automatic. With the manual switch, you have to decide which computer has the "right of way" to print and flip the switch to the position for that computer.

With an automatic printer switch, the switch monitors incoming signals for documents to be printed, manages the print queue, and ensures that documents get printed in the order they were received.

In this exercise, you will make a printer available to all of the computers connected to your home network.

BE SURE TO connect a printer to your computer before beginning this exercise.

1   Click **Start**, and then click **Printers and Faxes**.

2   In the Printers and Faxes window, right-click the icon for the printer that you want to share, and then click **Sharing**.

Troubleshooting   If printer sharing has never been enabled on the computer, you might need to go through the Network Setup Wizard before following the rest of the steps.

3   On the **Sharing** tab of the printer **Properties** dialog box, select the **Share this printer** option.

Troubleshooting   If you're still unable to share the printer or continue with the steps as listed below, click the **Start** button, click **Control Panel**, click **Network and Internet Connections**, and then click **Windows Firewall**. In the **Windows Firewall** dialog box, click the **Exceptions** tab, select the **File and Printer Sharing** check box, and then click **OK**.

4   In the **Share name** box, type Wallace Family Printer, and then click **OK**.

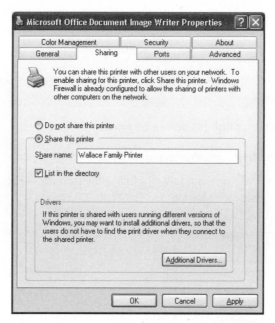

5 To stop sharing a network printer, click **Start**, and then click **Printers and Faxes**.

6 In the Printers and Faxes window, right-click the icon for the printer that you want to discontinue sharing, and then click **Sharing**.

7 On the **Sharing** tab of the **Properties** dialog box, select the **Don't share this printer** option, and then click **OK**.

Sharing a Network Folder

If you have more than one computer, you will probably want to share files between them. For example, your daughter might take a mobile PC to the library to research and write her history report, and then continue to work on the report later on a home desktop computer. If no home network is available, she will need to copy the document onto a floppy disk or other media, and from there onto the second computer.

By using a home network, you can give other network users permission to access files and folders stored on your mobile PC. You can copy or move files from one PC to another and not have to worry about the file sizes or drive availability. When you share a drive or a folder, you allow people to access the information whenever they need it as long as your computer is turned on.

In this exercise, you will share a folder and set the access permissions to that folder.

USE the *Yearly Sales Presentation* file in the practice file folder for this topic. This practice file is located in the *My Documents\Microsoft Press\Laptops and Tablet PCs with Windows XP SBS\AtHome \TransferringFiles* folder.

1 Click **Start**, and then click **My Documents**.

2 In the My Documents window, browse to the *Microsoft Press\Laptops and Tablet PCs with Windows XP SBS\AtHome* folder.

3 Right-click the **TransferringFiles** folder, and then click **Sharing and Security**.

4 In the folder **Properties** dialog box on the **Sharing** tab, select the **Share this folder** option.

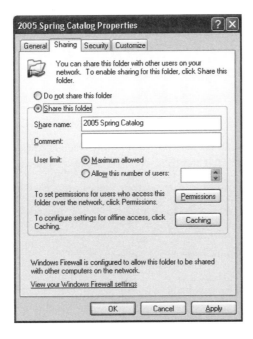

Important The **Sharing** option is not available for the Documents and Settings, Program Files, and WINDOWS system folders.

5 To set user permissions for the folder, click **Permissions**.

6 In the **Permissions for** dialog box in the **Allow** column, select the **Change** check box.

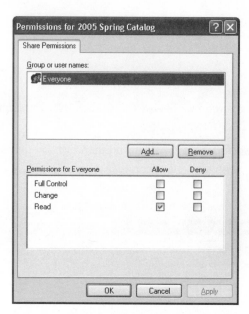

7 To share the folder with other users on your network, click **OK** twice.

8 On a different computer connected to the network, click **Start**, and then click **My Computer** to confirm that the folder is shared over the network.

9 In the My Computer window in the **Other Places** area, click **My Network Places**.

10 To view the contents of the shared folder, locate the shared folder, and then double-click it.

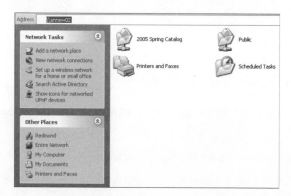

Close

11 To close the shared network folder window, click the **Close** button.

12 To stop sharing a network folder, click **Start**, and then click **My Documents**.

13 In the My Documents window, locate the shared folder, right-click it, and then click **Sharing and Security**.

14 In the **Properties** dialog box, on the **Sharing** tab, select the **Do not share this folder** option, and then click **OK**.

Moving Data Between Computers

When you use more than one computer or are upgrading to a newer, faster, or more powerful computer, you might need to move data from one computer to another. The Files and Settings Transfer Wizard helps you move both your data files and your personal settings between computers. For example, you can take your personal display properties, folder and taskbar options, and Internet browser and e-mail settings from one computer and transfer them to another. The wizard also moves specific files or entire folders, such as My Documents, My Pictures, and Favorites.

Important   Passwords are not moved with program settings when you use the Files and Settings Transfer Wizard. This is a security measure that helps to keep your passwords confidential.

In this exercise, you will transfer files and folders from one computer to another by using the Files and Settings Transfer Wizard.

USE the *Yearly Sales Presentation* file in the practice file folder for this topic. This practice file is located in the *My Documents\Microsoft Press\Laptops and Tablet PCs with Windows XP SBS\AtHome \TransferringFiles* folder.

1   Click **Start**, point to **Programs**, point to **Accessories**, point to **System Tools**, and then click **Files and Settings Transfer Wizard**.

2   On the first page of the Files and Settings Transfer Wizard, click **Next**.

Important   If either the source computer or the destination computer is running an earlier version of Windows, insert the Windows XP Professional CD into the CD-ROM drive, click **Perform Additional Tasks** on the **Welcome** menu, and then click **Transfer Files and Settings** to start the Files and Settings Transfer Wizard.

3 On the **Which computer is this?** page, select the **Old Computer** option, and then click **Next**.

| Unblock |

Important If a Windows Security Alert message box appears, click the **Unblock** button to continue running the wizard.

4 On the **Select a transfer method** page, select the **Home or small office network** option, and then click **Next**.

5 The next page lets you determine exactly what you want transferred: settings, files or both. Browse to the *My Documents\Microsoft Press\Laptops and Tablet PCs with Windows XP SBS\AtHome\TransferringFiles* folder, double-tap **2005 Fall Catalog**, and then select **Yearly Sales Presentation**.

Now go to the other PC you want to transfer files to and repeat the process.

6 On the **Which computer is this?** page, select the **New Computer** option, and then click **Next**.

If the computers are networked, the destination computer automatically starts receiving the files.

7 When you're done, click **Finish**.

Connecting to a Virtual Private Network

If you would like to be able to connect to your corporate network, either from home or while on the road, and your organization has set up a remote access server, you can create a virtual private network (VPN) connection to your corporate network and have full use of network resources while you are away from the office. A VPN connection uses the Internet to access a private (corporate) network, thus extending the private network and enabling your computer to operate as though it were physically connected to the network.

Important Some companies do not permit users to take company-issued mobile PCs home for fear of a security risk to both the information stored on the computer and the computer itself (because it could be stolen or misplaced). Some corporations also do not permit users to connect their personal computers to the office network or check e-mail remotely.

In this exercise, you will create a VPN connection to The Garden Company's corporate network.

BE SURE TO know your user account name and password as well as the host name or IP address of your organization's remote access server before you begin this exercise.

Troubleshooting You won't be able to complete this exercise if you don't have access to a remote access server (RAS).

1 Click **Start**, and then click **Control Panel**.

2 In Control Panel, click the **Network and Internet Connections** link.

3 In the Network and Internet Connections window, click **Create a connection to the network at your workplace**.

4 On the **Network Connection** page, select the **Virtual Private Network connection** option, and then click **Next**.

5 On the **Connection Name** page in the **Company** box, type The Garden Company, and then click **Next**.

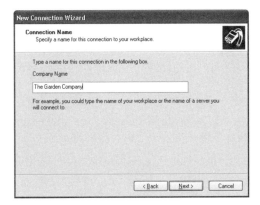

6 On the **Public Network** page, select the **Do not dial the initial connection** option, and then click **Next**.

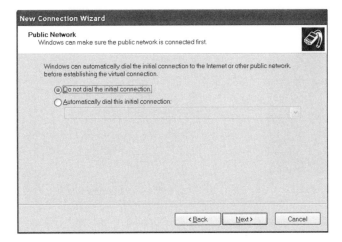

7 On the **VPN Server Selection** page, type the host name or IP address for your company's remote access server, and then click **Next**.

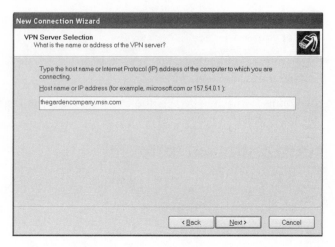

8 If you have a smart card, on the **Smart Cards** page, make sure that the **Do not use my smart card** option is selected, and then click **Next**.

9 On the **Connection Availability** page, make sure that the **My use only** option is selected, and then click **Next**.

10 On the **Completing the New Connection Wizard** page, click **Finish**.

11 To test the newly created VPN connection, in the Network and Internet Connections window, click **Network Connections**.

12 In the Network Connections window, double-click the icon representing the connection you just created.

13 In the **Connect The Garden Company** dialog box, type your user name and password, and then click **Connect**.

When you are connected to the network, a network icon appears in the notification area, and you can connect to the same network resources as you could if you were sitting at your desk at work.

14 To close the VPN connection, right-click the network icon in the notification area, and then click **Disconnect**.

15 To delete the VPN connection, in the Network Connections window, right-click the icon representing the VPN connection, and then click **Delete**.

16 When prompted to confirm the deletion, click **Yes**.

CLOSE the Network Connections window.

Accessing Your Office Computer by Using Remote Desktop

When working from home or another remote location, you might need to access files or even programs that are stored on your desktop computer in the office. With Remote Desktop, you can have access to a Windows session that is running on your office computer while using another computer. For example, you can leave programs running at work before heading home and then use Remote Desktop to access your office computer from your mobile PC or home computer and pick up where you left off.

When you connect to your office computer remotely, Remote Desktop locks that computer to prevent anyone from accessing programs and files stored on it. When you get back to your work computer the next morning, simply unlock the computer by pressing [Ctrl]+[Alt]+[Del] and then typing your password.

To use Remote Desktop, you need the following:

■ A computer running Windows XP Professional ("remote" computer) with a connection to a LAN or the Internet.

■ A second computer (home or mobile computer) with access to the LAN through a network connection, modem, or VPN connection. The second computer must have Remote Desktop Connection, formerly called the Terminal Services client, installed. Remote Desktop ships as part of Windows XP Professional.

■ Appropriate user accounts and permissions.

In this exercise, you will enable your work computer to be accessed through Remote Desktop, and then start a Remote Desktop connection on your mobile PC.

BE SURE TO set up your office computer or the computer you want to access remotely to allow remote connections, and log on to your office computer as an administrator to enable the Remote Desktop feature before you begin this exercise.

1 To enable Remote Desktop on your office computer, click **Start**, and then click **Control Panel**.

2 In Control Panel, click **Performance and Maintenance**.

3 In the Performance and Maintenance window, click **System**.

4 In the **System Properties** dialog box, click the **Remote** tab.

5 In the **Remote Desktop** area, select the **Allow users to connect remotely to this computer** check box, and then click **OK**.

6 To start a Remote Desktop session, click **Start**, point to **All Programs**, point to **Accessories**, point to **Communications**, and then click **Remote Desktop Connection**.

7 In the **Remote Desktop Connection** dialog box, type the name or the IP address of your work computer.

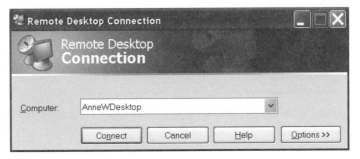

Close

8 To end the session, click the **Close** button on the Remote Desktop window title bar.

Troubleshooting Remote Desktop disconnected your session because you did not send a response within the set time limit or because of a slow connection caused by excessive network traffic, try connecting to the office computer again. If you're unable to re-establish the connection, contact your network administrator.

Speech Recognition on Your Tablet PC

If you use a Tablet PC, you can create documents or add text and comments to existing documents by using your voice. The Tablet PC Input Panel (TIP) has speech recording capabilities that allow both dictation, in which your spoken words are converted to text, and voice commands, in which your words open menus and activate on-screen buttons as well as switch between programs. When you are in a quiet environment, such as an office or a hotel room, the power of speech can help you dictate a document or reply to e-mail messages by using the combination of speech and ink.

Before you can record your voice as text, you must train the system to recognize your speech patterns. Also note that anyone with a strong regional or foreign accent might see lower recognition results unless the system is trained. The more time you spend teaching the system, the better the recognition will be.

In this exercise you will train your Tablet PC to recognize your voice.

BE SURE TO have a boom microphone or a headset that is designed for use with your Tablet PC available before beginning this exercise.

1 Tap the **Tablet PC Input Panel** icon.

2 On the right side of the Tablet PC Input Panel, tap the **Tools and Options** button, and then tap **Speech**.

The first time you tap this command, you are prompted to train the system to recognize your voice.

3 In the **Speech Recognition Enrollment** dialog box, tap **Next**.

The Microphone Wizard Welcome page appears.

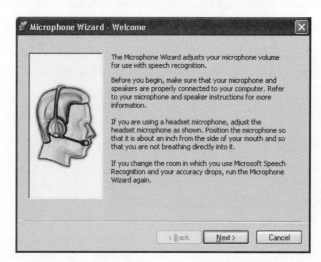

4   On the **Microphone Wizard Welcome** page, follow the instructions to adjust your microphone, and then click **Next**.

5   Read the paragraphs aloud.

The words recognized by the system will be highlighted.

6   Click **Next**.

A Dictation button and a Command button appear in the Tablet PC Input Panel.

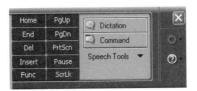

7   To test the speech functionality, tap **Start**, tap **All Programs**, tap **Accessories**, and then tap **WordPad**.

8   Press and hold the **Dictation** button in the Table PC Input Panel and then say **This is a test**.

Tip   If you want to spell out a word, say "spell it" and then immediately being spelling the word. The letters appear as you say them until you pause, at which point the system reverts to normal dictation mode.

9   When you're finished speaking, release the **Dictation** button.

10   Click the **Close** button.

11   Tap the **Tablet PC Input Panel** icon to minimize it.

Key Points

■   You can share files, printers, and Internet connection between computers across your home network.

■   While at home, you can access corporate resources by using virtual private network (VPN), and access computers at your workplace by using Remote Desktop.

■   You can dictate a document by using Speech Recognition functionality on a Tablet PC.

Play a music CD on a mobile PC, page 132

Transfer music to a mobile PC, page 137

Listen to Internet radio on a mobile PC, page 141

Transfer digital photographs to a mobile PC, page 146

Chapter 7 at a Glance

7 At Home: Playing and Sharing Digital Media

In this chapter you will learn to:

✔ Familiarize yourself with Windows Media Player.

✔ Play a music CD on a mobile PC.

✔ Transfer music to a mobile PC.

✔ Listen to Internet radio on a mobile PC.

✔ Watch a DVD on a mobile PC.

✔ Copy music to a portable device.

✔ Transfer digital photographs to a mobile PC.

✔ Connect a mobile PC to a home entertainment system

Some people might think of the mobile PC solely as a useful work tool, but they're missing a great opportunity to use it also as a portable entertainment device. You can play games, music, and movies, as well as store and view digital photographs wherever you are.

In this chapter, you will learn how to use Microsoft Windows Media Player 10 on your mobile PC to view, listen to, and share digital media that you can enjoy while you are at home or on the road.

See Also Do you need only a quick refresher on the topics in this chapter? See the Quick Reference entries on pages xxxiii–xxxvi.

Familiarizing Yourself with Windows Media Player

Windows Media Player 10 and Microsoft Windows XP are a great combination for enjoying music and video on your computer. You can play CDs and DVDs, download new music, listen to the radio over the Internet, and much more.

Windows Media Player 10 includes several new features that make it even better than previous versions for viewing and sharing media on your mobile PC. Some of the key features are:

- *Digital music playback.* Windows Media Player 10 can play different types of music files including CDs, *MP3s*, and Windows Media Audio (WMA) files.

- *Burning CDs.* If your mobile PC supports CD-RW, you can compile your favorite music tracks and create your own CDs with Windows Media Player 10.

■ *Media Library.*   Windows Media Player 10 provides a central catalog of all the music and video files stored on your PC. You can search and sort for media by a variety of categories, such as album name, artist, and genre.

■ *DVD playback.*   If your mobile PC supports DVD (as most new computers do), you can watch your favorite DVDs by using Windows Media Player 10.

■ *Smart Jukebox.*   When you're ready to listen to music, you can let Windows Media Player 10 select which tracks to play based on your listening habits and preferences. For example, you can specify that you want to hear a random selection of music tracks that you have recently added to your *Media Library.*

■ *Online Stores.*   Windows Media Player 10 provides links to several Web sites where you can buy and download music to listen to.

■ *Digital audio player synchronization.*   You can connect a digital audio player to your mobile PC and use Windows Media Player 10 to copy music files to the audio player so that you can listen to them away from your computer.

Tip   For more information about Windows Media Player 10, including the list of supported digital audio players, see *www.microsoft.com/windows/windowsmedia/.*

Playing a Music CD on a Mobile PC

Windows Media Player is a great music player that you can use to quickly find the music you want to play, and easily control the playback of music when it is playing.

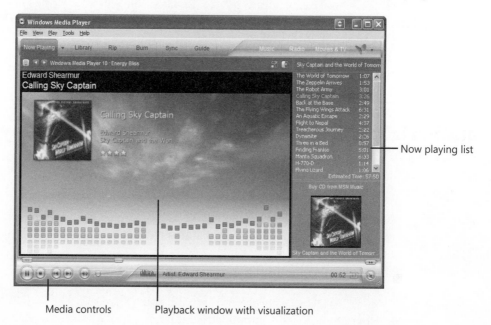

Now playing list

Media controls   Playback window with visualization

You can use Windows Media Player in four different modes:

■ *Full Screen.* In this mode, the playback window fills the entire screen. The playlist area is hidden, and the Windows taskbar and media controls only appear when the pointing device (the mouse or the tablet pen) is moved.

■ *Full Mode.* In this mode, the title bar, media controls, and playlist are visible, and you can resize the player as you can any other program window.

■ *Skin Mode.* This mode displays smaller versions of the playback area and media controls. Different "skins" are available, which you can use to change the way the player looks.

■ *Mini Mode.* This mode displays only the media controls, on the Windows taskbar, and is ideal for listening to music while you are performing other tasks on your computer.

In this exercise, you will play music, create a playlist, change the visualization of the music you're listening to, and try out the various playback modes available in Windows Media Player.

BE SURE TO install Windows Media Player 10 or later, have a music CD available, and connect to the Internet before beginning this exercise.

> **Tip** You can download the latest version of Windows Media Player from *www.microsoft.com/windows/windowsmedia/*.

1 Click **Start**, point to **All Programs**, and then click **Windows Media Player**.

Windows Media Player opens in Full Mode and, if this is the first time you have used Windows Media Player, starts playing a sample music track.

2   Open the optical drive tray on your mobile PC and insert a music CD.

See Also   For more information on optical drives, see "Understanding Storage Devices" in Chapter 2, "Getting to Know Your Mobile PC Hardware."

---

3   Click the **Now Playing** down arrow, and then click **CD Drive**.

4   The list of tracks from the CD appears in the Now Playing List, the CD starts to play through your speakers, and a visualization moves in time to the music in the playback area.

Windows Media Player then searches an online database of CDs and, if you are connected to the Internet, retrieves the track name and album art for the CD. Only the list of track titles or other album details will display if you're not connected to the Internet or information can't be found.

Troubleshooting   If no sound or music can be heard from your mobile PC's speaker, try moving the Windows Media Player volume slider to the right to ensure that the volume has not been turned down or muted. If you still can't hear any music, click **Start**, click **Control Panel**, click **Sounds, Speech and Audio Devices**, and then click **Adjust the system volume**. In the **Sounds and Audio Devices Properties** dialog box, make sure that the **Mute** check box is cleared, and then move the **Device volume** slider to the right. If this doesn't fix the problem, consult the manufacturer's documentation to locate your mobile PC's volume control and mute button.

5   To modify the visualization, right-click the playback area, point to **Musical Colors**, and then click **Colors in Motion**.

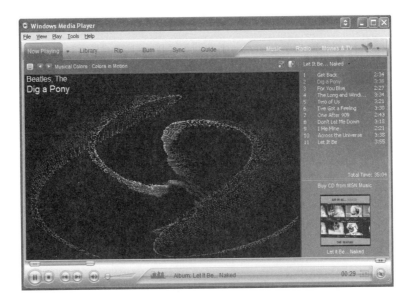

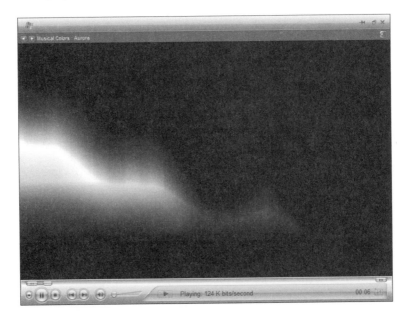

6 To change the visualization again, click the **Next visualization** button.

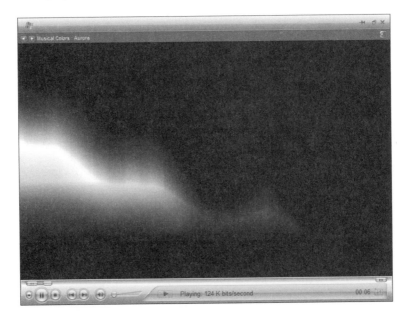

Next
visualization

7 On the toolbar, click the **View Full Screen** icon.

The media controls and the toolbar disappear when the pointing device stops moving for a couple of seconds.

View Full
Screen

8 To display the media controls and the toolbar again, move the pointing device.

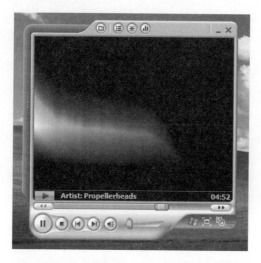

Exit Full Screen

9 To return Windows Media Player to Full Mode, click the **Exit Full Screen** button.

10 On the **View** menu, click **Skin Mode**.

Tip Windows Media Player comes with a variety of skins, but you can also download additional skins from the Internet. To see skins that you can download, click the **Tools** menu, click **Download**, and then click **Skins**.

11 Right-click the playback window, and then click **Switch To Full Mode**.

12 To view Windows Media Player in Mini Mode, right-click the Windows taskbar, point to **Toolbars**, and then click **Windows Media Player**.

Minimize

13 To minimize Windows Media Player, click the **Minimize** button.

Windows Media Player now appears as a toolbar on the Windows taskbar.

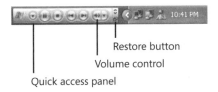

Restore button

Volume control

Quick access panel

Tip   If you hover with your pointing device over the Mini Player, information about the currently playing track is displayed.

Restore

14   To restore Windows Media Player to Full Mode, click the **Restore** button on the Mini Player.

15   Click the **Close** button.

Close

Understanding Codecs and Audio Compression

Windows Media Player takes the music from a CD and uses a special algorithm, called a *codec*, to compress the music into smaller files that are easier to store and manage. Windows Media Player 10 can rip music by using the WMA and MP3 codecs.

See Also   For more information about the quality differences between WMA and MP3 codecs, visit *www.microsoft.com/windows/windowsmedia/demos/audio_quality_demos.aspx*.

Music tracks are compressed by reducing the quality of the audio. The higher the quality, the more file space is necessary. Before you start copying (or ripping) CDs, think about the trade-off between quality and size that you will need to make. By default, Windows Media Player 10 will rip music in WMA format at 64 Kbps. This usually is acceptable if you intend to listen to the music through headphones or small speakers, but you might want to increase the rip rate to 96 Kbps to get slightly higher quality.

Transferring Music to a Mobile PC

In addition to playing back music from a CD, you can also copy the tracks from your favorite CDs and store them on your mobile PC's hard disk, which makes carrying around a pile of CDs with you a thing of the past. The process of copying music from a CD to your mobile device is commonly known as *ripping* the CD.

In this exercise, you will use Windows Media Player to rip a CD to your mobile PC.

BE SURE TO have a music CD available before beginning this exercise.

1   Insert the music CD into the optical drive of your mobile PC.

The **Audio CD (D:)** dialog box appears.

2   In the **What do you want Windows to do** area, click **Play audio CD using Windows Media Player**.

Windows Media Player opens and the CD starts playing.

3   On the taskbar, click the **Rip** tab to display details about each of the tracks on the CD.

If you are connected to the Internet and the music CD you are playing was found in the online database, the track details are filled in for you, including the album name, track name, composer, and genre.

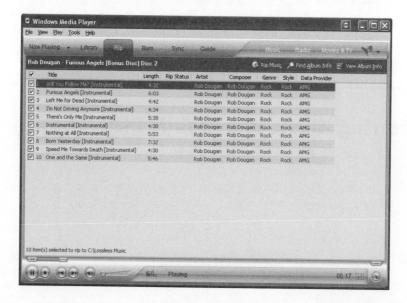

Troubleshooting   If track details are incorrect, select the track with the erroneous information, right-click the selected information, click **Edit**, and then type the correct data. If no information about your music CD was found in the online database, click the **Find Album Info** button and either click **Search** to search the online database, or click **Edit** to type information that you know to be accurate.

Tip   You can choose to not rip a specific track by clearing the check box to the left of the track title.

4   When you are ready to start ripping the CD, press the **Rip Music** button.

The Rip Status column displays the progress of each track as it is ripped to the computer hard disk.

Tip   By default, the copied music is placed in the My Music folder. To access the default storage location, codec, or compression level settings, click the **Tools** menu, click **Options**, and in the **Options** dialog box, click the **Rip Music** tab.

5 When your CD has been ripped, click the **Library** tab and take a look at the contents of the Media Library to ensure that all the desired tracks were copied.

6 To expand the list of available albums, in the Media Library, click **Album**.

7 From the album that you just ripped, right-click one of the tracks, and then click **Add to Now Playing List**.

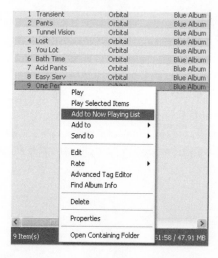

8   The selected track is now queued to play.

9   To see the list of tracks that are going to play, click the **Now Playing** tab, and then look at the list displayed in the pane on the right.

>   **Tip**   You can use the media controls to play, pause, or skip to the next or previous track.

10   After you have finished, click the **Close** button.

Close

Understanding Playlists

A playlist is a list of songs and videos that you can access through your Media Library. You can turn Windows Media Player 10 into your own jukebox by selecting a list of songs from any album, and then saving that list to play back later. You can create as many lists as you want and each list can contain any number of tracks. To create a playlist, right-click the tracks that you want to include, and then click **Add to Now Playing List** (as in step 7 above).

Listening to Internet Radio on a Mobile PC

You can not only listen to music you have purchased as CDs or from a Web site, but you can also use Windows Media Player 10 to listen to the radio. You can listen to hundreds of radio stations from around the world, not just the local stations you can receive on your car radio.

In this exercise, you will use Windows Media Player to listen to a radio station.

BE SURE TO have a working Internet connection before beginning this exercise.

1   Click **Start**, and then click **Windows Media Player**.

2   On the Windows Media Player taskbar, click the **Radio** tab.

The playback area displays a list of available radio stations.

Tip You can also search for a particular radio station or type of music.

3 To open the current list of international radio stations, click the icon to the left of **International**.

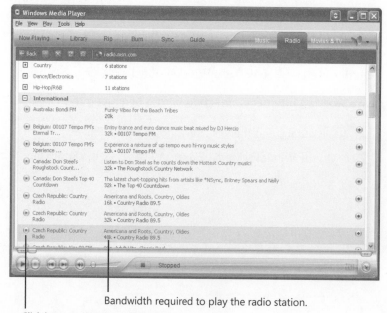

Bandwidth required to play the radio station.

Click here to play the radio station.

Play

4 Select a radio station, and then click the **Play** icon.

A live broadcast of the selected radio station can be heard.

Troubleshooting If you are not using a broadband Internet connection, you might not be able to listen to all of the radio stations. If you're unable to hear the radio station you selected, pick a different radio station with a lower bandwidth, and then try again.

Close

5 Click the **Close** button.

Watching a DVD on a Mobile PC

If your mobile PC has a DVD drive, you have everything you need to turn your PC into a portable DVD player. In order to use Windows Media Player 10 as a DVD player, you will need to purchase DVD decoder software. This software is usually included when you purchase a new mobile PC (see your manufacturer's documentation for details). If it is not included, many distributors sell the decoder software.

See Also For more information about decoder software and DVD support, visit *www.microsoft.com/windows/windowsmedia/windowsxp/dvdplay.aspx*.

In this exercise, you will use Windows Media Player 10 to play a DVD on your mobile PC.

BE SURE TO have a DVD available before beginning this exercise.

1 Insert the DVD into the DVD drive of your mobile PC.

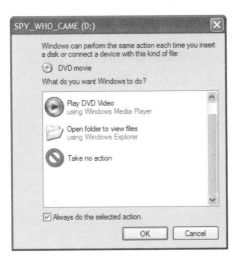

Troubleshooting   If the **Autoplay** dialog box does not appear, start Windows Media Player manually by clicking **Start**, and then clicking **Windows Media Player**.

2   In the **Autoplay** dialog box, click **Play DVD using Windows Media Player**.

Windows Media Player opens and starts playing the DVD.

Note   DVD content often looks better when played in Full Screen mode. You can change to Full Screen mode by pressing ⌐Alt¬+⌐Enter¬, or by clicking on the **View** menu, and then selecting **Full Screen**.

3   When you have finished watching the DVD, click the **Close** button.

Close

Copying Music to a Portable Device

When you want to listen to music but are not planning on taking your mobile PC, you can copy music from Windows Media Player 10 to a portable device such as a digital audio player, a PDA, or a cell phone. These types of portable devices usually have a limited amount of storage space available to copy music files to, so you can usually only copy part of your Music Library.

In this exercise, you will copy a music album to a portable device.

BE SURE TO have a portable device that can play back digital music, such as a **Pocket PC**, a **cell phone**, or a **digital audio player** before beginning the exercise.

See Also   For a list of compatible devices, see *www.microsoft.com/windows/windowsmedia /devices/default.aspx*.

---

1   Click **Start**, and then click **Windows Media Player**.

2   Plug your portable device into your mobile PC.

Tip   The portable device is usually connected via a USB cable or cradle.

3   The Device Setup dialog box appears.

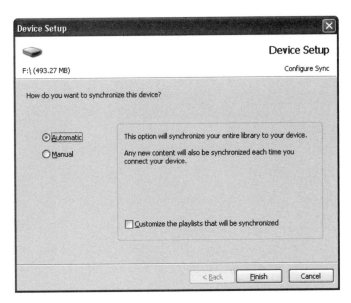

If your portable device has more than 512 MB of storage, the option will be set to **Automatic**; otherwise, it will be set to **Manual**.

When the **Automatic** option is selected, Windows Media Player 10 will copy the latest files to the device when you plug it in. If there is not enough space on the device for all of the files in your Media Library, the media will be synchronized based on your preferences.

Note You can build your own Sync media list that will be copied to the device by using Manual synchronization. You can add to the Sync list by right-clicking the item you want to add, and then clicking **Add to Sync List**.

4 In the **Device Setup** dialog box, select the **Automatic** option, and then click **Finish**.

Tip If you want to change the settings used to define what is automatically synchronized, connect your device to the mobile PC, click the **Sync** tab in Windows Media Player, and then click **Sync Settings**. In the **Synchronization Settings** dialog box, you can configure what will be synchronized by selecting or clearing the appropriate check boxes.

5 Windows Media Player starts synchronizing the files to your portable device. You can track the progress in the Sync List.

Note You can stop the synchronization at any time by pressing the **Stop Sync** button.

Close

6 When the synchronization is complete, unplug your device, and then click the **Close** button.

Transferring Digital Photographs to a Mobile PC

Digital cameras have revolutionized the way people take and share photographs. You no longer have to wonder how the photo you took will come out because you can see the results immediately. You can also store and view the pictures on your computer, edit them if necessary (for example, remove red eye or change the brightness of the picture), send copies of pictures to family and friends in an e-mail message, and print high-quality copies.

Because your mobile PC is easy to take with you wherever you go, it makes the perfect vacation companion for your digital camera.

In this exercise, you will transfer pictures from your digital camera to your mobile PC.

BE SURE TO have a digital camera available that is compatible with Windows XP and has pictures stored on it before beginning this exercise.

Troubleshooting If this is the first time you have connected your camera to your mobile PC, you will need to install the driver software necessary for Windows XP to "talk" to your camera. Consult the manufacturer's documentation and follow the instructions to install the driver.

1 Connect your digital camera to your mobile PC.

The digital camera Plug and Play dialog box appears, prompting you to select which program you would like to use to download the pictures from your camera.

2 Click **Microsoft Scanner and Camera Wizard**, and then click **OK**.

3 On the first page of the Microsoft Scanner and Camera Wizard, click **Next**.

4 On the Choose Pictures to Copy page, select the check boxes corresponding to the pictures that you want to copy to your mobile PC, and then click **Next**.

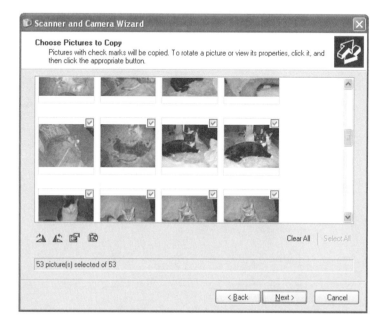

5 On the Picture Name and Destination page, type a name in the **Type a name for this group of pictures** box, and then click **Next**.

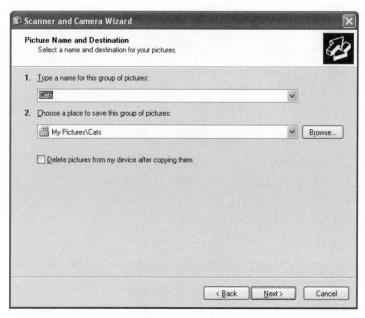

6 The pictures download from the digital camera to your mobile PC.

7 On the Other Options page, select the **Nothing. I'm finished working with these pictures** option, and then click **Next**.

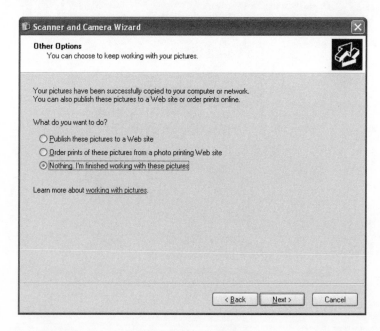

8   Click **Finish**.

9   Click **Start**, and then click **My Pictures**.

10   In the My Pictures window, double-click the folder that you created in step 5.

       The digital pictures you just copied from your digital camera are listed.

Next Image

11   To view the next picture in the list, click the **Next Image** button.

12   In the **Picture Tasks** area, click **View as a slide show**.

       Your pictures are shown full screen, one after the other.

13   When you have finished viewing your pictures, press the [Esc] key on your keyboard, and then click the **Close** button.

Close

Sharing Digital Pictures on the Internet

You can easily share your digital pictures by posting them to a Web site so that others can view them over the Internet. This is a great way to share photos with friends and family. To publish your pictures to a Web site:

1   Start the Microsoft Scanner and Camera Wizard, and then click **Next**.

2   On the Choose Pictures to Copy page, select the check boxes corresponding to the pictures that you want to copy to your mobile PC, and then click **Next**.

3   On the Picture Name and Destination page, type a name in the **Type a name for this group of pictures** box, and then click **Next**.

4 On the Other Options page, select the **Publish these pictures to a Web site** option.

5 On the Change Your File Selection page, select the list of pictures that you want to share, and then click **Next**.

6 On the Where do you want to publish these files? page, select the Web site provider you want to use to share your pictures.

Windows XP provides a link to MSN Groups, but you can use any provider that you like. If you choose MSN Groups, follow the instructions to create a mini Web site, name it, and then set access privileges, such as whether you want everyone to able to see the pictures, or just a list of people that you define. You can then access and view your pictures from the MSN Groups Web site.

Connecting a Mobile PC to a Home Entertainment System

If you want to show your photos to several people in a room, listen to your digital music on more powerful speakers, or watch a DVD on a larger screen, you might want to connect your mobile PC to your stereo equipment or television. Your mobile PC usually has audio outputs that can be used to connect it to a stereo. It might also have a video output that you can use to connect it to a television.

See Also For more information about identifying the audio and video outputs on your mobile PC, see Chapter 2, "Your Laptop and Tablet PC Hardware."

Connecting to a Stereo System

To connect your mobile PC to a stereo, you will need a cable that connects the 1/8″ stereo headphone jack on your computer to the RCA audio inputs on your stereo. These cables are cheap and readily available from most electronics stores. Your stereo system will usually have two *RCA phono jacks*, one red and one white (often labeled *External In*).

After you have connected the cable, any sound coming from your computer will be piped through your stereo system speakers. You can use Windows Media Player to play the music from your Music Library (as described earlier in this chapter), as well as create custom playlists—ideal for parties!

Connecting to a Television

Some mobile PCs have a TV output. These outputs take one of four forms:

- Composite video. A single RCA phono jack (usually yellow). This gives the lowest picture quality but is supported by almost all television sets.

- S-Video. A small round jack with multiple pins. This gives better picture quality than composite video and is also supported by most television sets.

- Component video. Three RCA phono jacks (usually red, green, and blue). This is just starting to appear on mobile PCs and gives a high-quality video image that is designed to connect to an *HDTV*.

- DVI. A rectangular socket with multiple pins. This is a new, very high-quality way to connect your mobile PC to an external monitor or HDTV.

See Also   For more information about identifying which of these TV output options your mobile PC has, see "Identifying Laptop Ports and Jacks" in Chapter 2, "Getting to Know Your Mobile PC Hardware."

Before trying to connect your mobile PC to your television, you will need to assess which of the options listed above are supported by your equipment, and then if necessary, purchase the appropriate connector cables.

After you have connected the television to your mobile PC into the appropriate connector, consult your mobile PC manufacturer's documentation and follow the instructions necessary to enable your PC to send an image to your television, because it is different for each manufacturer.

Troubleshooting   Depending on the type of television you are connecting to, you might need to adjust the screen resolution of your mobile PC. A standard television can usually support a screen resolution of only 640x480; an HDTV can support a much higher resolution.

Windows XP Media Center Edition on Mobile PCs

Windows XP Media Center Edition is a new version of Windows XP that enables you to record television programs on your computer and watch them later, as well as view photos and listen to music on your television, and control it all with a special remote control. Some computer manufacturers offer laptops that run Windows XP Media Center Edition. These laptops are perfect for small apartments or dorm rooms where it can be your television, your stereo system, your DVD player, and your PC—all in one convenient unit.

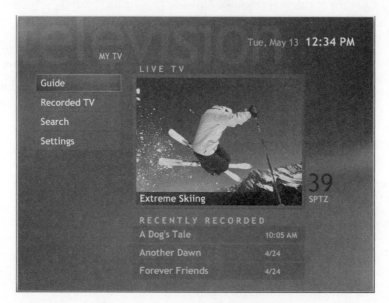

If you have a desktop version of Windows XP Media Center Edition at home, you can copy your recorded TV programs onto your mobile PC and watch them when you are away from home by using Windows Media Player 10.

See Also   For more information about Windows XP Media Center Edition, visit *www.microsoft.com/mediacenter/*.

Key Points

- Using Windows Media Player 10, you can listen to a CD, or listen to radio stations from around the world, on your mobile PC.

- You can rip the music from a CD to your computer's hard disk so that you can listen to it without having to carry the CD with you.

- Your mobile PC is a great way to play DVDs.

- With a digital camera, you can store images on your mobile PC.

- You can connect your mobile PC to a stereo system so that you can listen to music on more powerful speakers.

- You can connect your mobile PC to a TV so that you can watch a DVD on a larger screen, or display a slideshow of your digital photographs to other people.

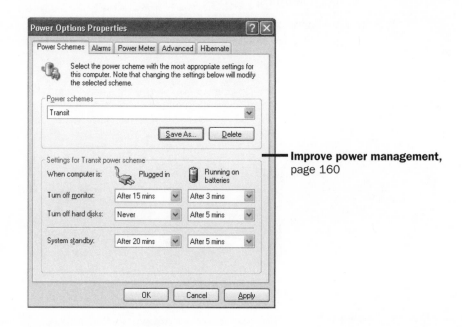

Improve power management,
page 160

Chapter 8 at a Glance

8 Traveling with Your Mobile PC

In this chapter you will learn to:

✔ Connect to a public network.

✔ Understand 3G networks.

✔ Operate a mobile PC during a flight.

✔ Improve power management.

When you take trips, either for business or for pleasure, you can remain productive by working on your mobile PC, connecting to the Internet from public networks, or you can take a well-deserved break and watch a DVD while on a cross-country flight.

In this chapter, you will learn how to optimally travel with your mobile PC by connecting to public networks and new 3G mobile networks, and how to use your computer as an entertainment device while saving battery power.

See Also Do you need only a quick refresher on the topics in this chapter? See the Quick Reference entries on pages xxxvi–xxxvii.

Connecting to a Public Network

When you travel with a mobile computer, you can connect to the Internet through wireless networks installed in many public places, such as airports or hotels. The networking concepts and safety precautions you learned in Chapter 3, "Introduction to Networking," will be useful when you connect to the Internet from public places while traveling.

Wireless networks provide high-speed Internet access that is available to anyone with a Wi-Fi–enabled mobile PC or handheld device. These networks are usually public and give people on the go, whether in their neighborhood or across the world, the opportunity to connect to the Internet, send and receive e-mail messages, get directions to a store or a museum, or post restaurant reviews after a satisfying dinner with friends.

One concern you might have about connecting to the Internet from a public place is security. Wireless Provisioning Services (WPS) in Microsoft Windows XP SP2 enables public wireless networks to provide a consistent sign-in and configuration experience, while providing more secure access to network resources.

When you connect to a wireless network that supports WPS, you are prompted to download setup files that are used to ensure a more secure, consistent, and automatic configuration. After you download the files, the Wireless Network Registration Wizard requests logon information from you—some networks might require payment, while others might only require acknowledgement of a usage policy.

Tip   Since WPS is a new feature in Windows XP SP2, not all public hotspots support this feature as of yet. As a result, you may be asked to go through the individual hotspot configuration to use wireless connection. The files required by WPS do not contain any personal information about you or your computer.

In this exercise, you will connect to a public wireless network.

BE SURE TO install Windows XP Service Pack 2 (SP2) on your mobile PC and locate a public wireless network that supports Wireless Provisioning Services (for example, a public wireless ISP such as those found at coffee shops) before beginning this exercise.

1   Click **Start**, and then click **Control Panel**.

2   In Control Panel, click **Network and Internet Connections**.

3   In the Network and Internet Connections window, click **Network Connections**.

4   In the Network Connections window, click the **Wireless Network Connection** icon.

5   In the **Network Tasks** area, click **View available wireless networks**.

6   In the Wireless Network Connection window, click **Find a wireless network location** under **Related Tasks**.

7   Complete the fields to search for a wireless public Internet service provider (ISP) in a specific location.

The more information that you provide, the more precise the search will be.

Understanding 3G Networks

Cellular phones allow us to talk to people while on the road. Advancements in cellular technology now allow mobile PCs to offer third generation (3G) mobile services. In simple terms, 3G services combine high-speed wireless access with Internet Protocol (IP)–based services. This also allows for new ways to communicate, access information, conduct business, learn, and be entertained.

Cellular carriers believe that 3G will become the norm for many communication services. You will be able to make video calls and browse the Internet simultaneously, or play interactive games with friends. 3G allows for both convenience and speed of access. Typically with 3G's ability of "anytime access," you are charged by the amount of information you send and receive, rather than the amount of time you are connected.

The following table compares the technologies used by and the features associated with the existing three network generations:

Generation	Technology	Features
1G	Advanced Mobile Phone Service (AMPS)	● Analog voice service ● No data service
2G	Code Division Multiple Access (CDMA) Time Division Multiple Access (TDMA) Global System for Mobile Communications (GSM)	● Digital voice service ● 9.6 Kbps to 14.4 Kbps. ● Not suitable for on-the-go data connection
3G	Wide-band Code Division Multiple Access (W-CDMA)	● Superior voice quality ● Up to 2 Mbps. always-on data ● Broadband video and multimedia data services
	CDMA with Data & Video (CDMA 1xEV-DV)	● Video conferencing (high quality) ● High-speed Internet

See Also   For more information about connecting to a 3G network, contact your mobile phone carrier. Most carriers offer a PC Card that can be plugged into your mobile PC for use with 2G and 3G cellular networks.

Tips for Traveling with a Mobile PC

Here are a few useful tips to keep in mind when you travel domestically and internationally with your mobile PC:

■ The hard disk drive is a sensitive component of your laptop and any information on your computer might be more valuable than the hardware, so keeping it safe is a priority. Your mobile PC should contain sensitive data only when it is essential for the trip. You might consider keeping sensitive data separate on a CD-ROM. Also, be sure to keep a backup copy of all important files at home or on a regularly backed up company server.

See Also   For more information about backing up your data, see "Backing Up Files and Folders" in Chapter 9, "Maintaining and Protecting Your Mobile PC."

- Carry your mobile PC on the plane with you; do not pack it in a suitcase or check it through with the rest of your luggage. It only takes a short drop or something moderately heavy being thrown on top of the computer to break the LCD panel. Mobile PCs are also temperature-sensitive and could be damaged by prolonged exposure to the cold temperatures typical in a cargo hold.

- Make sure your computer is fully charged, and then activate the Standby mode the last time you use it before going to the airport. Standby mode enables your mobile PC to restart quickly and consumes minimal battery power; the battery stays charged longer so that you can work during or while waiting for your flight. When you go through airport security, you might be asked to turn your computer on. Being able to start your computer quickly will help to avoid delays.

- Keep an eye on your mobile PC at all times. X-ray machines at airports are not a threat to your mobile PC's disk drives. However, the security checkpoint conveyer belts are frequented by thieves who watch for unattended equipment passing through the X-ray machines.

- Before plugging your modem into a hotel phone jack, ask the front desk staff whether it's safe. Many hotels use digital phone systems, which operate at a higher voltage than regular phone systems. These digital phone lines can damage your modem, and the manufacturer's warranty might not cover a replacement.

- When traveling internationally, your mobile PC's power adapter can handle the voltage in most countries—anything between 100 and 240 volts alternating current (AC) will work. You will, however, need to buy an outlet converter so that you can plug the power adapter into a wall outlet. You might also want to bring along a telephone cord and adapter as well as a phone line filter (if you're visiting countries that use tax impulses on the phone lines such as Germany, Spain, and Switzerland).

- Verify that none of the software installed on your computer is illegal in your destination country. If you are unsure about encrypted software on your system, consult your system administrator.

- For more information about encryption software restrictions, visit *www.bxa.doc.gov /encryption/* or consult the import/export agencies of the countries or regions in which you are traveling.

Operating a Mobile PC During a Flight

Many airplanes are now equipped with power and wireless networks for passengers to use during a flight. In the coming years, passengers will come to expect these capabilities whenever they step on a plane. If you are currently in the market for extra batteries for in-flight use, instead consider a power adapter designed for use with the in-flight power systems.

Some commercial airlines request that you turn off portable computers during certain portions of the flight, such as takeoff and landing. To comply with this request, you must turn off your computer completely. Putting your computer in Standby mode won't do the trick because, even though your computer might appear to be turned off, the operating system might reactivate itself to run pre-programmed tasks or to conserve battery power. To prevent this from occurring during air travel, shut down your computer completely when not in use.

If your computer is equipped with a cellular modem, you must ensure that the modem is completely turned off during air travel as required by Federal Communications Commission regulations. Failure to comply with these requirements could lead to civil or criminal penalties.

In this exercise, you will turn off wireless networking on your mobile PC.

BE SURE TO log on to your mobile PC before beginning this exercise.

1   Click **Start**, and then click **Control Panel**.

2   In Control Panel, click **Network and Internet Connections**.

3   In the Network and Internet Connections window, click **Network Connections**.

4   In the Network Connections window, right click the **Wireless Network Connection** icon, and then click **Disable**.

Tip   Some mobile PCs have a physical button or switch to turn on or off the wireless connection. Refer to your manufacturer's documentation for more details.

Improving Power Management

You might not give much thought to the battery that powers your mobile PC until it runs out at an inopportune moment—such as when you're putting the finishing touches on a PowerPoint presentation during a flight to a client meeting. However, there are steps you can take to improve the power efficiency of mobile devices.

You have probably heard the term "power management" before, and you might have wondered what it meant and why it seems to be so important for mobile devices in general and mobile PCs in particular. In a nutshell, the term *power management* refers to the steps you can take to reduce power to components that aren't being used. Good power management can double or triple the life of a battery.

The default Windows XP configuration provides good power management. If you're interested in fine-tuning the settings, here are some ways you can optimize your battery power:

- A spinning hard drive can certainly drain battery power. So, by setting the hard drive to turn off at a certain point, for instance three minutes, you save significant power.

See Also   For more information about hard disk drives, see "Understanding Storage Devices" in Chapter 2, "Getting to Know Your Mobile PC Hardware."

- Reduce the level of backlighting and dim your screen. On color systems, you can save quite a bit of power by changing to black-and-white (monochrome) mode.

- Avoid running graphically intensive programs, such as games. Watching movies doesn't drain your battery as much as you might think because spinning the DVD drive isn't as bad as spinning the hard drive.

- Take advantage of Intel SpeedStep if you're using a mobile PC with an Intel processor (Pentium III or greater). SpeedStep cycles down the processor on newer Intel-based computers when you're mobile. For example, if you have a 2 GHz Pentium 4 laptop, it cycles down to 1.2 GHz when you're running on batteries.

- Turn off the modem, if not needed, and remove any PC Cards not in use.

- If you don't plan on using the battery for a month or more, store it in a clean, dry, cool place away from heat and metal objects. NiCd, NiMH, and LiIon batteries self-discharge during storage.

- Turn off the monitor when not in use: It consumes more power than any other mobile PC component.

Battery Dos and Don'ts

You can extend battery life and power to the mobile PC using software settings as described in the previous section, but taking good care of the battery itself is also critical.

Battery Dos: A new battery comes in a discharged condition and must be charged before use. Upon initial use or after a prolonged storage period, the battery might require several charge/discharge cycles before achieving maximum capacity.

- When charging a battery for the first time, the device might indicate that charging is complete after just 10 or 15 minutes—a normal phenomenon with rechargeable batteries. Remove the battery from the device, reinsert it, and repeat the charging procedure.

- It is important to condition (fully discharge and then fully charge) the battery every two to three weeks. Failure to do so might significantly shorten the battery's life.

- If the battery will not be in use for a month or longer, remove it from the device and store it in a cool, dry, clean place.

- It is normal for a battery to become warm to the touch during charging and discharging.

- Actual battery run-time depends on the power demands made by the equipment. A notebook computer's battery life depends on screen brightness and the use of the CPU, the hard drive, and other peripherals.

- The total run-time of the battery is heavily dependent on the design of the equipment. To ensure maximum performance of the battery, optimize the computer's power management features.

- For more information about managing battery power, see "Getting More Power Out of Your Battery" in Chapter 5, "Using Your Mobile PC in Meetings.""

Battery Don'ts:

- Do not drop, hit, or otherwise abuse the computer; this could result in the exposure of the corrosive cell contents.

- Do not expose the battery to moisture or rain.

- Keep the battery away from fire or other sources of extreme heat. Incinerating or exposing the battery to extreme heat might result in an explosion.

Optimizing Battery Power

You can reduce the power consumption of your computer hardware, or of your entire system, by choosing a *power scheme*—a collection of settings that manages your computer's power usage. You can create your own power schemes, or use those provided with Windows XP.

In this exercise, you will explore one of the built-in power schemes and then create a custom one.

BE SURE TO log on to Windows before beginning this exercise.

1 Click **Start**, and then click **Control Panel**.

2 In Control Panel, click **Performance and Maintenance**.

3 In the Performance and Maintenance window, click **Power Options**.

4 In the **Power Options Properties** dialog box, click the **Power scheme** down arrow, and then click **Max Battery**.

Review the default settings after you choose this scheme.

5 To create a custom power scheme based on this built-in scheme, in the **Running on batteries** area, click the **Turn off monitor** down arrow, and then from the list, click **3 minutes**.

6 Click the **Turn off hard disk** down arrow, and then in the list, click **5 minutes**.

7 To save these settings as a new power scheme, click **Save As**.

8   In the **Save Scheme** dialog box, type Transit, and then click **OK**.

9   To select another built-in power scheme, click the **Power scheme** down arrow, and then click **Portable/Laptop**.

10   To apply the currently selected power scheme, click **OK**.

11   Click the **Close** button.

Close

Key Points

■ While traveling, you can connect your mobile computer to the Internet through wireless networks installed in many public locations, such as hotels or airports, and over 3G networks.

■ You can extend your battery life and optimize your mobile PC functionality while using the battery by following a few key steps.

■ Use your laptop for productivity and entertainment while in flight.

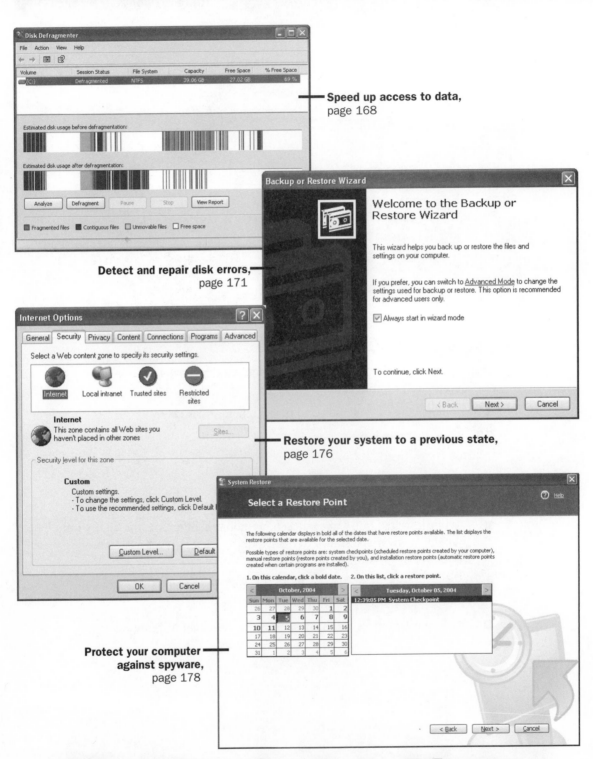

Speed up access to data,
page 168

Detect and repair disk errors,
page 171

Restore your system to a previous state,
page 176

Protect your computer
against spyware,
page 178

Chapter 9 at a Glance

9 Maintaining and Protecting Your Mobile PC

In this chapter you will learn to:

✔ Clean your computer.

✔ Free up disk space.

✔ Speed up access to data.

✔ Detect and repair disk errors.

✔ Back up files and folders.

✔ Restore your system to a previous state.

✔ Protect your computer against spyware.

There are a few housekeeping tips that you should keep in mind to maintain your mobile PC. In addition to protecting your computer against attacks from the Internet, you want to perform regular maintenance and cleaning of your PC to keep your system running smoothly. With Windows XP Service Pack 2 (SP2), you have better protection against viruses, hackers, and worms, as well as access to system tools that you can run periodically to optimize your computer's performance.

In this chapter, you will learn how to use the tools provided in Windows XP Service Pack 2 (SP2) to safeguard your privacy when you're online, free up disk space by clearing out unnecessary files, create a back-up of your files, and restore your system from that back-up if needed. You will also learn simple tips for cleaning your mobile PC.

See Also   Do you need only a quick refresher on the topics in this chapter? See the Quick Reference entries on pages xxxvii–xxxix.

Cleaning Your Computer

If you want your mobile PC to stay in good working order, you should clean it regularly. You not only need to clean your computer's drive disk, but also its screen, mouse, keyboard, and any and all fans and ports. A little regular maintenance will go a long way toward preventing major hardware failures.

Your computer's two worst enemies are heat and moisture. Excess heat accelerates the deterioration of the delicate circuits in your system. Overheating is most often caused by dust and dirt; clogged vents and cooling fans can keep air from circulating properly, and even a thin coating of dust or dirt can raise the temperature of your computer's components.

Before you begin to clean your computer, have the following supplies handy:

- Rubbing alcohol
- Compressed air (16-ounce can)
- Clean, lint-free white cloths
- Cotton swabs—the longer the better
- A small vacuum
- LCD wipes

When you have the necessary supplies ready, shut down your mobile PC, disconnect any attached devices (such as mice and external CD drives), and unplug any attached cord from the electrical outlet.

Follow these instructions to clean the specific parts or accessories of your computer:

- Case: Wipe the front and back panels of the case and use compressed air to clear any vents. Be careful not to blow dust into the computer or its disk drives.
- Mouse: If you have an attached non-optical mouse, unscrew the ring on the bottom of the mouse and remove the ball. Scrape the accumulated dirt and deposits off the two plastic rollers inside the ball's housing. If you have an optical mouse, simply blow off any dust that may have accumulated below the surface of the mouse.
- Touch pad: Moisten a soft, lint-free cloth with water, and then stroke it gently across the surface of the touch pad. Do not allow water from the cloth to seep between the touch pad and the surrounding palm rest.
- Keyboard: Turn the keyboard upside down and shake it to clear any debris stuck from between the keys. If that's not enough, use compressed air to finish the job. If the keys are really dirty, or stick when you press them, pry them off with a dampened cloth for easier cleaning.

- LCD Screen: Clean the screen with LCD cleaner (available at a computer store) or with isopropyl alcohol if approved by your computer manufacturer. Wipe your LCD lightly because the underlying glass is fragile.

- CDs and DVDs: Gently wipe each disc with a moistened, soft cloth. Use a motion that starts at the center of the disc and then moves outward toward the edge. Never wipe a disc in a circular motion.

Freeing Up Disk Space

The Disk Cleanup tool is a utility that ships with Microsoft Windows and helps you free up space on your hard disk by identifying files that you can safely delete. You can choose to delete some or all of the identified files.

Use Disk Cleanup to do the following:

- Remove temporary Internet files.

- Remove downloaded program files (such as Microsoft ActiveX controls and Java applets).

- Empty the Recycle Bin.

- Remove Windows temporary files.

- Remove optional Windows components that you don't use.

- Remove installed programs that you no longer use.

In this exercise, you will run Disk Cleanup on your mobile PC to identify and delete unneeded files, freeing up disk space and improving computer performance.

BE SURE TO log on to Windows as an administrator before beginning this exercise.

1   Click **Start**, point to **All Programs**, point to **Accessories**, point to **System Tools**, and then click **Disk Cleanup**.

Important   If several drives are available, you might be prompted to specify which drive you want to clean.

Disk Cleanup calculates the amount of space you will be able to free.

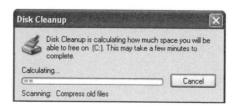

2   In the **Disk Cleanup for** dialog box, scroll through the content of the **Files to delete** list.

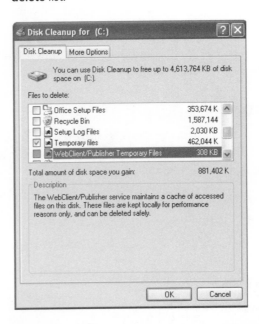

Tip   Typically, temporary Internet files take the most amount of space because the browser caches each page you visit for faster access later.

3   Clear the check boxes in front of files that you don't want to delete, and then click **OK**.

4   When prompted to confirm that you want to delete the specified files, click **Yes**.

After a few minutes, the process completes and the Disk Cleanup dialog box closes, leaving your computer cleaner and performing better.

Speeding Up Access to Data

As you create and delete files and folders, install programs, or download files from the Internet, your computer saves these files in the first contiguous free space that is large enough to accommodate it. If your computer doesn't have a large enough section of free space for the file, the computer saves as much of it as possible in the largest available space and then saves the remaining data in the next free space, and so on. As a volume fills up with file and folder storage, new files are saved in pieces across the volume. When you delete files, the empty spaces left behind fill in randomly as you store new files. This is known as disk fragmentation.

Over time, fragmentation slows down disk access and degrades the overall performance of the system. When files are fragmented, the computer must search the hard disk each time the file is opened to piece it back together, causing the response time to be significantly longer.

Disk Defragmenter is a Windows utility that consolidates fragmented files and folders on your computer's hard disk so that each occupies a single, contiguous space on the disk. With your files stored neatly end-to-end, without fragmentation, reading and writing to the disk speeds up.

In this exercise, you will run Disk Defragmenter on your mobile PC to gather all the scattered file fragments on your hard disk and write them into adjacent clusters so that each file occupies a contiguous section of the disk.

BE SURE TO log on to Windows as an administrator before beginning this exercise.

1 Click **Start**, point to **All Programs**, point to **Accessories**, point to **System Tools**, and then click **Disk Defragmenter**.

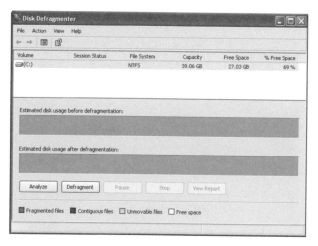

2 In the **Disk Defragmenter** dialog box, click the drives that you want to defragment, and then click the **Analyze** button.

Tip You should analyze a volume before defragmenting it to get an estimate of how long the defragmentation process will take.

After the disk is analyzed, a dialog box appears, informing you whether you need to defragment.

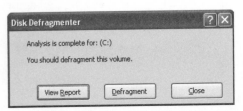

3 If the result of the analysis advises you to defragment the drive, click the **Defragment** button.

After the defragmentation is complete, Disk Defragmenter displays the results.

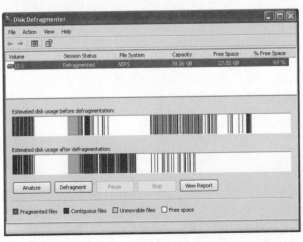

4 To display detailed information about the defragmented disk or partition, click **View Report**, and then click the **Close** button on the View Report window.

Close

5 To close the Disk Defragmenter utility, click the **File** menu and then click **Exit**.

When to Run Disk Defragmenter

In addition to running Disk Defragmenter at regular monthly intervals, certain events warrant running the utility outside of the monthly rule of thumb.

You should run Disk Defragmenter in the following circumstances:

■ You add a large number of files. Volumes can become excessively fragmented when you add a large number of files or folders, so be sure to analyze volumes after this happens.

■ Your free disk space nears 15 percent. A volume must have at least 15 percent free space for Disk Defragmenter to completely and adequately defragment. Disk Defragmenter uses this space as a sorting area for file fragments. If a volume has less than 15 percent of free space, Disk Defragmenter will only partially defragment it. To increase the free space on a volume, delete unneeded files using Disk Cleanup or move them to another disk.

■ You install new programs or a new version of Windows. Volumes often become fragmented after installing programs, so running Disk Defragmenter helps to ensure the best file system performance possible.

Detecting and Repairing Disk Errors

In addition to running Disk Cleanup and Disk Defragmenter to optimize the performance of your mobile PC, you can investigate the integrity of the files stored on your hard disk by running the Error Checking utility.

When you use your hard drive, it can develop bad sectors. Bad sectors tend to spread when Windows tries to write data to them, eventually slowing down hard disk performance and sometimes making data writing (such as file saving) difficult, or even impossible.

The Error Checking utility scans the whole partition or drive for bad sectors and scans for file system errors to see whether certain files or folders are misplaced. Sooner or later, hard disks get bad sectors. If you use your computer daily, you should try to run this utility weekly to help prevent data loss.

In this exercise, you will run the Error Checking utility on your mobile PC to search for and identify any bad sectors on your hard disk, and then attempt to recover them if any exist.

BE SURE TO close all files before running the Error-Checking utility for this exercise.

Troubleshooting   If the volume is currently in use, you will be prompted to indicate whether you want to reschedule the disk checking for the next time you restart your system. Then, when you do restart your system, disk checking will run and the disk will not be available to perform other tasks while this process is running.

1 Click **Start**, and then click **My Computer**.

2 In the My Computer window, right-click the hard disk you want to search for bad sectors, and then click **Properties**.

3 In the dialog box that appears, click the **Tools** tab.

4 Click the **Check Now** button.

5   In the **Check Disk** dialog box, select the **Scan for and attempt recovery of bad sectors** check box, and then click **Start**.

Tip   Only select the **Automatically fix file system errors** check box if you think that your disk contains bad sectors.

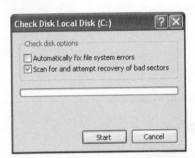

6   If bad sectors are found, choose to fix them.

Note   If your drive is formatted as NTFS, Windows logs all file transactions, replaces bad clusters, and stores copies of key information for all files on the NTFS volume.

Backing Up Files and Folders

Just as you need to take care of the hardware that stores your data, you also need to protect your files and folders from accidental loss in case of hardware or storage media failure.

Using the Backup utility that comes with Windows XP, you can create a duplicate copy of the data on your hard disk and then archive the data on another storage device. The backup storage medium can be a drive on your computer or a separate storage device, such as a removable disk. If the original data on your hard disk is accidentally erased or overwritten, or becomes inaccessible because of a hard disk malfunction, you can easily restore the data from the archived copy.

The Backup utility creates an accurate point-in-time copy of the contents of your hard disk, including any open files or files that are being used by the system. You can use the Backup utility to accomplish the following:

■   Archive selected files and folders on your hard disk, and then restore them to your hard disk or any other accessible disk.

■   Schedule regular backups to keep your archived data up-to-date.

■   Use Automated System Recovery to save and restore all the system files and configuration settings needed to recover from a complete system failure.

■   Make a copy of your computer's system partition, boot partition, and the files needed to start up your system in case of computer or network failure.

Important You can also use Backup to back up and restore data on either the file allocation table (FAT) or NTFS file system volumes. However, if you have backed up data from an NTFS volume used in Windows XP, you should restore the data to the same type of volume and Windows structure. If you do not, you could lose data, as well as some file and folder features such as permissions.

In this exercise, you will back up the contents of your My Documents and Favorites folders, as well as your desktop settings and any saved cookies, and then you will restore the backed up files.

BE SURE TO log on as an administrator before beginning this exercise.

Troubleshooting If you are a member of the Users or Power Users group, you must be the owner of the files and folders you want to back up, or you must have one or more of the following permissions: Read, Read and Execute, Modify, or Full Control.

1 Click **Start**, point to **All Programs**, point to **Accessories**, point to **System Tools**, and then click **Backup**.

The Backup or Restore Wizard appears.

2 On the first page of the Backup or Restore Wizard, click **Next**.

3 On the **Backup or Restore** page, make sure that the **Back up files and settings** option is selected, and then click **Next**.

4 On the **What to Back Up** page, make sure that the **My documents and settings** option is selected and then click **Next**.

5 On the **Backup Type, Destination, and Name** page, click the **Browse** button.

6 In the **Save As** dialog box, click the **Save in** down arrow, and then click **Desktop**.

7 To name the backup file, click in the **File name** box, type' test, and then click **Save**.

8 On the **Backup Type, Destination, and Name** page, click **Next**.

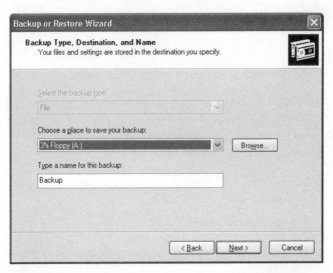

9 To back up the selected files and settings, click **Finish**.

The Backup Progress dialog box appears. The backup process takes anywhere from a few minutes to several hours, depending on the size of the folders and files that you are backing up.

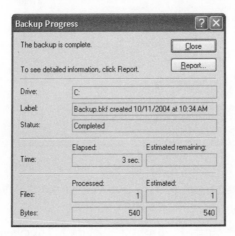

10 To close the **Backup Progress** dialog box, click **Close**.

A backup file icon appears on your desktop.

11 To restore the files, folders, and settings, click **Start**, point to **All Programs**, point to **Accessories**, point to **System Tools**, and then click **Backup**.

12 On the first page of the Backup or Restore Wizard, click **Next**.

13 On the **Backup or Restore** page, select the **Restore files and settings** option, and then click **Next**.

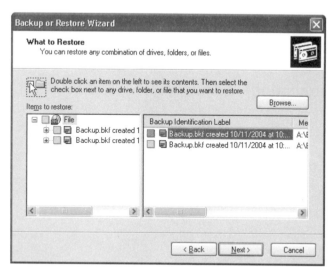

14 On the What to Restore page, click the plus sign to the right of the **File** icon, click the plus sign to the right of **Test.bfk**, select the **C:** check box, and then click **Next**.

15 To restore the backed up files and settings, click **Finish**.

The restore process takes the same amount of time as the backup process.

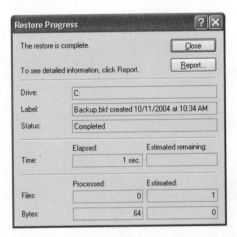

16 To close the **Restore Progress** dialog box, click **Close**.

Restoring Your System to a Previous State

You can also use Windows System Restore to undo harmful changes to your computer and restore its settings and performance. System Restore monitors changes to the system and some program files, and creates easily identified restore points daily. Using restore points, you can revert the system to a previous time. If you know the date that the computer functioned properly, you can restore your computer to the previous state without losing your personal data files (such as Microsoft Word documents, browsing history, drawings, favorites, or e-mail messages).

Troubleshooting You must have Windows XP Professional or Windows XP for Tablet PC Edition to run System Restore on your mobile PC.

In this exercise, you will restore the system to a previous state.

BE SURE TO log on as an administrator before beginning this exercise.

1 Click **Start**, point to **All Programs**, point to **Accessories**, point to **System Tools**, and then click **System Restore**.

The System Restore Wizard appears.

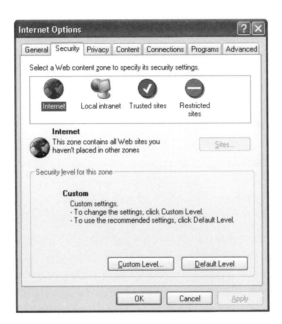

2   Click **Next**.

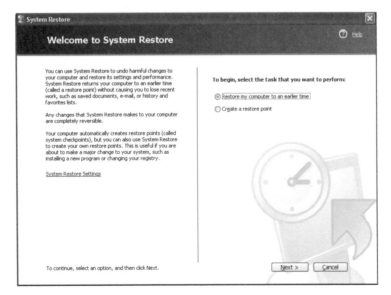

3   On the calendar, select a date in bold for the restore point.

4   Click **Next** twice.

Your computer restarts with data from the restore point.

Protecting Your Computer Against Spyware

Spyware is a new type of software that collects personal information without letting you know and without asking for permission. The information that spyware collects ranges from a list of Web sites that you visit to usernames and passwords. You significantly increase your risk of being the target of spyware if you download free games from Internet sites you don't trust or download programs from unknown sources or publishers.

Spyware is associated often with software that displays advertisements, called adware. Some advertisers covertly install adware on your system and generate a stream of unsolicited advertisements that can clutter your desktop and affect your productivity. The extra processing required by your computer to track your browsing habits or to display advertisements can tax your computer and hurt your system performance.

Not all software that provides ads or tracks your online activities is bad. For example, if you sign up for a free Internet service, you might receive in return targeted advertisements for companies that offer free services. Likewise, tracking online activities can be useful when displaying customized search content or personalized preferences at an online retailer.

One way you can try to prevent software from silently installing on your system without any warning is to adjust the security settings used by your Web browser. By keeping the Security level at medium or high, you can better control what is installed on your computer.

In this exercise, you will adjust the security settings used by Internet Explorer for different content zones.

BE SURE TO log on to your computer before beginning this exercise.

1 Click **Start**, and then click **Internet Explorer**.

2 In Internet Explorer, click the **Tools** menu, and then click **Internet Options**.

3 In the **Internet Options** dialog box, click the **Security** tab.

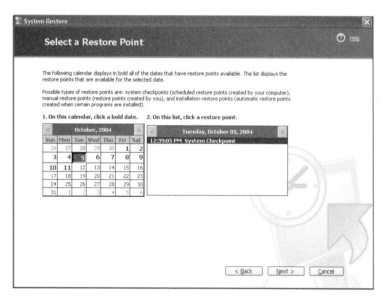

4   In the **Select a Web content zone to specify its security settings** area, click **Internet**.

5   In the **Security level for this zone** area, click **Default Level**.

6   To ensure safe and functional Web surfing while still preventing unsigned ActiveX controls from downloading, move the slide up to **Medium** and then click **OK**.

How to Spot Spyware Running on Your Computer

It is likely that spyware is running on your computer if you notice any or all of the following problems:

- When you start your Web browser, it opens to a page you've never seen before.

- You are noticing a sudden increase in advertisements on pages where you've never seen them before.

- Your computer seems slow.

Different companies provide a variety of tools to detect and remove unwanted software from your computer. To view some of the tools available, visit *www.microsoft.com /athome/security/spyware/default.mspx*.

Key Points

■ Back up your data on a regular basis.

■ Protecting and maintaining your mobile PC on a regular basis ensures the longevity of your hardware and keeps your computer fast and error- free.

■ Browsing the Internet can cause your computer to be infected by spyware. To prevent spyware from infecting your computer, run anti-spyware software regularly and adjust security settings for Internet Explorer.

■ Restore your system from a known restore point if you notice suspicious computer behavior or encounter problems after installing a program.

Glossary

ad hoc wireless network   A private network set up between two or more computers.

bandwidth   The transfer capacity of data over a network. Units of measurement are typically in numbers of bits per second.

Bluetooth   A type of wireless communication with a range of about 30 feet that can be used to communicate with compatible devices, such as some cell phones

broadband connection   A high-speed connection such as DSL, cable modem, or 3G cellular network.

cable modem   A device that connects to cable television lines to provide Internet access.

ClearType   A Microsoft technology that improves the readability of text on a LCD screen.

cloned mode   See *mirrored mode*.

codec   Short for *c*ompressor/*dec*ompressor. A codec is an algorithm used to compress and decompress data. MP3 and WMA are examples of codecs.

convertible   A type of Tablet PC that has a keyboard and can be converted into a slate by rotating the display.

cookie   A small file that is stored on your computer containing information about a Web site that you have visited. Information in the cookie typically contains your username or password.

defragmentation   The process of rewriting parts of files on a disk to increase the speed of access and retrieval.

Digital Subscriber Line (DSL)   A technology for delivering a broadband Internet connection over a telephone line.

dock   A device that extends the hardware capabilities of a mobile PC, including the number of ports.

domain name   The name that identifies a Web site. For example, "microsoft.com" is the domain name of Microsoft's Web site.

Domain Name System (DNS)   An Internet service that converts a domain name (such as *www.microsoft.com*) into an IP address.

DVD   A type of optical disk that can store a large amount of data. DVDs often contain movies or other video content. Many mobile PCs can playback DVDs.

Digital Visual Interface (DVI)   A high-quality cable that transfers images from a mobile PC to a compatible display (such as a monitor or HDTV).

Ethernet   A very common method of networking computers in a LAN using copper cabling. Ethernets handle about 10,000,000 bits-per-second and can be used with almost any kind of computer, including mobile PCs.

extended desktop mode   A feature of Microsoft Windows XP that extends the Windows desktop across two or more screens at the same time, effectively turning them into one large screen.

Fast User Switching   A method of quickly switching between users that are logged into Windows without having to log off and log on each time. This does not work on computers that are part of a network domain.

File Transfer Protocol (FTP)   A protocol for uploading and downloading files between various computers.

firewall   A security mechanism that prevents unauthorized access to computers.

gateway   A node on a network that serves as an entrance to another network. In enterprises, the gateway is the computer that routes the traffic from a workstation. In homes, the gateway is the ISP that connects the user to the internet.

High Definition Television (HDTV)   A new type of television set with a very high quality image.

Hypertext Transfer Protocol (HTTP)   The protocol for moving hypertext files across the Internet which requires a HTTP client program on one end, and an HTTP server program on the other end.

Integrated Services Digital Network (ISDN)   An international communications standard for sending voice, video, and data over digital telephone lines or normal telephone wires. ISDN supports data transfer rates of 64 Kbps (64,000 bits per second).

Internet Connection Sharing (ICS)   A feature in Windows that allows multiple computers to use a single connection to the Internet.

Internet protocol (IP) address   An identifier for a computer or device on a TCP/IP network. Networks using the TCP/IP protocol route messages based on the IP address of the destination. The format of an IP address is a 32-bit numeric address written as four sets of numbers separated by periods. Each number can be zero to 255. For example, 1.160.10.240 could be an IP address.

laptop computer   A type of mobile PC that has a screen and a keyboard, and is small enough be used on your lap.

LCD   An abbreviation of *Liquid Crystal Display*. A digital display that uses liquid crystal cells that change reflectivity in an applied electric field and is used for portable computer displays and watches.

local area network (LAN) A computer network that spans a relatively small area. Most LANs are confined to a single building or group of buildings. However, one LAN can be connected to other LANs over any distance through telephone lines and radio waves.

mirrored mode A video mode that projects an exact copy of the content of your mobile PC screen onto a projector screen or other external display.

mobile PC A generic term for any computer that has its own battery and can be carried around, including notebooks, laptops, and Tablet PCs.

modem A device that enables digital data transmission to be transmitted over tele-communications lines.

MP3 The name of the file extension and also the name of the type of file for MPEG, audio layer 3. Layer 3 is one of three coding schemes which uses perceptual audio coding and psychoacoustic compression to remove all superfluous information (more specifically, the redundant and irrelevant parts of a sound signal).

network interface card Often abbreviated as NIC, an expansion board you insert into a computer so the computer can be connected to a network. Most NICs are designed for a particular type of network, protocol, and media, although some can serve multiple networks.

notification area In Microsoft Windows, the area at the far right end of the taskbar, which typically shows the time of day and status information about various system tasks and programs running.

optical drive A secondary storage medium for computers. Information is stored on high-density disks in the form of tiny pits "read" (and sometimes written) by laser.

PC Card A hardware token compliant with standards promulgated by the Personal Computer Memory Card International Association (PCMCIA) providing expansion capabilities to computers, including the facilitation of information security. A device roughly the size of a credit card that can be connected to a PC card port on a mobile PC to add a specific hardware function, such as a wireless network card.

PCMCIA See *PC Card*.

personal digital assistant (PDA) A handheld device that has personal organization applications, such as e-mail, calendar, and contacts, and often functions as a cellular phone, fax sender, and Web browser.

port replicator An attachment for a mobile PC that allows a number of devices such as a printer, a large monitor, and a keyboard to be simultaneously connected.

power schemes A group of preset power-management options. For example, you can set elapsed times for putting your computer on standby and for turning off your monitor and hard disk. You save these settings as a named power scheme.

PS/2   A type of port (or interface) that can be used to connect a mouse and a keyboard to a computer. The PS/2 port is sometimes called the mouse port.

Remote Desktop   A Windows XP feature that allows more than one user to have active sessions on a single computer.

ripping   Transferring music from a CD to a computer.

Shared folder   A folder that is accessible to other people on a network.

slate   A Tablet PC that does not have an attached keyboard and can only be operated with the Tablet PC pen.

socket   A method of communication between two processes. A socket is an identifier that the application uses to uniquely identify an end point of communications. The user associates a protocol address with the socket by associating a socket address with the socket.

subnet mask   A local bit mask (set of flags) that specifies which bits of the IP address specify a particular IP network or a host within a subnetwork. An IP address of 128.66.12.1 with a subnet mask of 255.255.255.0 specifies host 1 on subnet 128.66.12.0. The subnet mask determines the maximum number of hosts on a subnetwork.

speech recognition   The ability of Windows XP to convert spoken words to written text. An internal driver, called a *Speech Recognition engine*, recognizes words and converts them to text.

S-Video   A video format offering a higher quality signal than composite video, but a lower quality than component video. This mid-level format divides the signal into two channels—luminance and chrominance. Some mobile PCs have an S-Video connector that can be used to show the computer image on a compatible television.

Tablet PC   A wireless personal computer (PC) that allows a user to take notes using natural handwriting with a stylus or digital pen on a touch screen. A Tablet PC is similar in size and thickness to a yellow paper notepad and is intended to function as the user's primary personal computer as well as a note-taking device. Tablet PCs generally have two formats, a convertible model with an integrated keyboard and display that rotates 180 degrees and can be folded down over the keyboard; or a slate style, with a removable keyboard.

taskbar   The bar that contains the Start button and is typically at the bottom of your desktop.

Telnet   A protocol for remote computing on the Internet. It allows a computer to act as a remote terminal on another machine, anywhere on the Internet. This means that when you telnet to a particular host and port, the remote computer (which must have a telnet server) accepts input directly from your computer (which must have a telnet client) and output for your session is directed to your screen.

Transmission Control Protocol/Internet Protocol (TCP/IP)   A suite of protocols that defines the Internet. Originally designed for the UNIX operating system, TCP/IP software is now available for every major kind of computer operating system. To be connected to the Internet, your computer must have TCP/IP software.

USB   An abbreviation of *Universal Serial Bus*. USB is a standard for easily connecting external devices (such as digital cameras and scanners) to a PC.

VGA   Abbreviation of *Video Graphics Array*. A VGA cable is a common way to connect a PC to another display device, such as an external monitor or a projector.

virtual private network (VPN)   A network scheme in which portions of a network are connected through the Internet, but information sent across the Internet is encrypted. The result is a "virtual network," which is also part of a larger network entity. This allows users to privately share information over a public infrastructure. VPNs are often used to connect offices.

wide area network (WAN)   A network that spans the distance between buildings, cities, and even countries. WANs are LANs connected together using wide area network services from telecommunications carriers and typically use technologies such as standard phone lines, ISDN, or other high speed services.

Windows Mobile   An operating system developed by Microsoft and used in Pocket PCs and some cell phones.

Windows Media Audio (WMA)   A Microsoft proprietary audio codec used for recording and playing back digital music on a computer or compatible digital audio device.

Index

Numerics

3G services, 156
802.11 standards, 42

A

accessing files remotely, 126
ActiveSync, 71
ad hoc wireless network, xxvii, 37, 95, 181
adware, 178
analyzing volumes, 169, 170
antivirus software, xxi, 44, 46
archiving
    data, 172
    files, 172
    folders, 172
audio compression, 137
Automated System Recovery, 172
automatic printer switch, 116
Automatic Updates feature, 4

B

backing up data, xxxviii, 172
Backup utility, 172
backups, xxxviii, 173
    restoring, xxxviii, 173
    scheduling, 172
    storage medium, 172
bad sectors., 171
bandwidth, 181
basic laptop components, 11
battery, 13, 100
    charging, 161
    discharging, 161
    life, optimizing, 27, 102
    power, optimizing, 162
    power, optimizing. See also
        power management

protecting, 161
run-time, 161
Bluetooth, 42, 71, 181
    comparing to 802.11 standards, 42
boot partition, 172
broadband, 34, 35, 181
    connection options, 36
burning CDs, 131

C

cables, 82. See also VGA cables
CDs
    burning, 131
    music, playing, xxxiii, 132
    ripping, xxxiv, 137
Check Disk utility, xxxvii
cleaning, 166
    accessories, 166
    supplies, 166
ClearType, xix, 12, 181
cloned mode. See mirrored mode
codecs, 137, 181
communicating with others, 53
components, laptop 11
composite video, 15
compression, audio, 137
computers, naming, 112
connecting remotely, 126
convertible Tablet PC, 22, 181
cookies, 181
corporate network, 122
creating home networks, 113

D

data
    archiving, 172
    backing up, 172
    moving between computers, 121
    restoring, xxxviii, 173

speeding up access to, 168
transferring, 121
data, sharing
    between mobile PCs, 90
    with ad hoc wireless network, 95
    with infrared data transmission, 92
    with USB flash drive, 91
decoder software, DVDs, 143
dedicated ports, 14
defragmentation, 181
defragmenting, 169
descriptions, providing for computers, xxix, 112
detecting
    errors, 171
    spyware, 179
devices, storage, 16
dial-up connection, 34
dictation, 127
digital audio player, 20
    synchronization, 132
digital camera, xxxv, 20
digital music playback, 131
digital photographs
    sharing on the Internet, 149
    transferring to mobile PCs, xxxv, 146
Digital Subscriber Line (DSL), 181
Disk Cleanup, xxxvii, 167
Disk Defragmenter, xxxvii, 169
    when to run, 170
disk fragmentation, 168
disk space, freeing, 167
display adapter port, 15
DNS server, 33
docking stations, 19
    undocking from, 77
    using with a laptop, 19
    using with external monitors, 50
docks, 18, 181
domain name, 33, 181
Domain Name System (DNS), 181

DualView. *See* extended desktop
    mode
DVDs, 181
    decoder software, 143
    playback, 132
    watching, xxxv, 143
DVI, 15, 181

E

e-mail, accessing offline, 76
Error Checking, 171
errors
    detecting, 171
    repairing, 171
Ethernet, 182
extended desktop mode, xxi, xxv,
    xxvi, 50, 83, 182
    configuring, 85
    projecting a presentation with,
      85
external optical drives, 17
external storage drives, 16

F

Fast User Switching, 182
File Transfer Protocol (FTP), 33,
    182
files
    accessing remotely, 126
    archiving, 172
    fragmented, 169
    integrity of, 171
    offline, xxiv
    taking offline, 71
    transferring, xxxi
firewalls, xxi, 44, 45, 182
flying with mobile PCs, 158, 159
folders
    archiving, 172
    fragmented, 169
    offline, xxiv

    setting permissions, 118
    Shared, 184
    sharing, xxviii, xxx
    taking offline, 71
    transferring, xxxi
fragmentation, 169
freeing space on hard disks, 167
FTP.. *See* File Transfer Protocol
    (FTP)

G

gateway, 33, 182

H

handwritten messages
    ink, 64
    MSN Messenger and, 64
hard disk
    drives, 16
    freeing up space on, 167
    malfunction, 172
headphone jack, 15
hibernating, xx
Hibernate mode, 27
high-speed Internet access, 35
home network
    creating, 113
    printers, sharing, xxx
    sharing a printer, 116
    sharing an Internet connection,
      116
    wireless, xxix, 114
Hypertext Transfer Protocol
    (HTTP), 33, 182

I

ICS. *See* Internet Connection
    Sharing (ICS)
infrared data transmission, xxvii,
    92
infrastructure wireless network,
    37, 95
ink. *See* handwritten messages
Integrated Services Digital
    Network (ISDN), 182
Internet Connection Sharing
    (ICS), 116, 182
Internet radio, 141
Internet service provider (ISP), 33
Internet, connecting to, 33
IP address, xxi, 32, 182
ISDN. *See* Integrated Services
    Digital Network (ISDN)

J

jacks, identifying, 13

L

LANs. *See* local area networks
    (LANs)
laptop screen, 12
    using ClearType with, 12
liquid crystal display (LCD), 12,
    182
local area networks (LANs), 32,
    34, 183

M

maintenance, 165
manual printer switch, 116
Max Battery power scheme, 102

About the Authors

Andrew Fuller is a Lead Program Manager in the Windows division at Microsoft, where he is working on the next generation of Windows for Mobile PCs. With more than ten years of experience in the IT industry both in Europe and in the United States, he has the passion and experience to make mobile PCs more useful for people everywhere through education and innovation. Andrew enjoys tinkering with technology, reading about history, and is an avid digital media enthusiast. He lives in Redmond, Washington, with his wife and cats, where he deals with the persistent rain and wishes there were a better way to get cat hair off his clothes.

Ravipal Soin is a Lead Program Manager in the Windows division at Microsoft. Prior to incubating the Mobile PC group within Windows, he worked on the first release of Windows XP for Tablet PC Edition. He also has contributed to books about Microsoft products and published papers on software development and media playback. Having used laptops for over a decade for work and for entertainment, he is passionate about building products that help users stay productive. Given the daily demands of personal and professional life, Ravipal hopes this book will help people realize their potential at work, at home, and at play.

Self-paced training that
works as hard as you do!

Microsoft® Windows®
XP Step by Step
Deluxe, Second
Edition
ISBN: 0-7356-2113-6
U.S.A. $39.99
Canada $57.99

Microsoft Office
Project 2003 Step by
Step
ISBN: 0-7356-1955-7
U.S.A. $29.99
Canada $43.99

Microsoft Office Excel
2003 Step by Step
ISBN: 0-7356-1518-7
U.S.A. $24.99
Canada $35.99

Microsoft Office
FrontPage® 2003
Step by Step
ISBN: 0-7356-1519-5
U.S.A. $24.99
Canada $35.99

Information-packed STEP BY STEP courses are the most effective way to teach yourself how to complete tasks with the Microsoft Windows operating system and Microsoft Office applications. Numbered steps and scenario-based lessons with practice files on CD-ROM make it easy to find your way while learning tasks and procedures. Work through every lesson or choose your own starting point—with STEP BY STEP'S modular design and straightforward writing style, *you* drive the instruction. And the books are constructed with lay-flat binding so you can follow the text with both hands at the keyboard. Select STEP BY STEP titles also prepare you for the Microsoft Office Specialist credential. It's an excellent way for you or your organization to take a giant step toward workplace productivity.

Microsoft Press has other STEP BY STEP titles to help you get the job done every day:

Home Networking with Microsoft Windows XP
Step by Step
ISBN: 0-7356-1435-0

Microsoft Office Word 2003 Step by Step
ISBN: 0-7356-1523-3

Microsoft Office Outlook 2003 Step by Step
ISBN: 0-7356-1521-7

Microsoft Office System Step by Step—2003
Edition
ISBN: 0-7356-1520-9

Microsoft Office PowerPoint 2003 Step by
Step
ISBN: 0-7356-1522-5

Microsoft Office Access 2003 Step by Step
ISBN: 0-7356-1517-9

To learn more about the full line of Microsoft Press® products, please visit us at:

microsoft.com/mspress

What do you think of this book? We want to hear from you!

Do you have a few minutes to participate in a brief online survey? Microsoft is interested in hearing your feedback about this publication so that we can continually improve our books and learning resources for you.

To participate in our survey, please visit:

www.microsoft.com/learning/booksurvey

And enter this book's ISBN, 0-7356-2170-5. As a thank-you to survey participants in the United States and Canada, each month we'll randomly select five respondents to win one of five $100 gift certificates from a leading online merchant.* At the conclusion of the survey, you can enter the drawing by providing your e-mail address, which will be used for prize notification *only*.

Thanks in advance for your input. Your opinion counts!

Sincerely,

Microsoft Learning

Microsoft | Learning

Learn More. Go Further.

To see special offers on Microsoft Learning products for developers, IT professionals, and home and office users, visit: *www.microsoft.com/learning/booksurvey*